Artificial Intelligence, Counter-Terrorism and the Rule of Law

Artificial Intelligence, Counter-Terrorism and the Rule of Law

At the Heart of National Security

Arianna Vedaschi

Full Professor of Comparative Public Law, Bocconi University, Italy

Chiara Graziani

Assistant Professor of Comparative Public Law, Bocconi University, Italy

Edward Elgar PUBLISHING

Cheltenham, UK • Northampton, MA, USA

Published by
Edward Elgar Publishing Limited
The Lypiatts
15 Lansdown Road
Cheltenham
Glos GL50 2JA
UK

Edward Elgar Publishing, Inc.
William Pratt House
9 Dewey Court
Northampton
Massachusetts 01060
USA

Authorised representative in the EU for GPSR queries only: Easy Access System Europe – Mustamäe tee 50, 10621 Tallinn, Estonia, gpsr.requests@easproject.com

A catalogue record for this book
is available from the British Library

Library of Congress Control Number: 2025932736

This book is available electronically in the **Elgar**online
Law subject collection
https://doi.org/10.4337/9781803928340

MIX
Paper | Supporting responsible forestry
FSC® C013604

ISBN 978 1 80392 833 3 (cased)
ISBN 978 1 80392 834 0 (eBook)

Printed and bound by CPI Group (UK) Ltd, Croydon, CR0 4YY

Contents

Figures

Acknowledgments

The authors would like to thank funding from MIUR - PRIN Bando 2020 - prot. 2020M47T9C 'Decision-Making in the Age of Emergencies: New Paradigms in Recognition and Protection of Rights.'

The authors would also like to thank the Baffi Research Center at Bocconi University for hosting the project.

The authors split the chapters as follows:

Introduction chapter: The introduction of this work is the result of shared thoughts between the two authors.

Part I Overview: This overview is the result of shared thoughts by both authors.

Chapter 1: Arianna Vedaschi authored sections 2 and 4; Chiara Graziani authored sections 1 and 3.

Chapter 2: Arianna Vedaschi authored sections 1 and 3; Chiara Graziani authored section 2.

Part I Final Overview: This final overview is the result of shared thoughts between the two authors.

Part II Overview: This general overview is the result of shared thoughts between the two authors.

Chapter 3: Arianna Vedaschi authored section 2.1; Chiara Graziani authored sections 1 and 2.2.

Chapter 4: Arianna Vedaschi authored section 2.2; Chiara Graziani authored sections 1 and 2.1.

Chapter 5: Arianna Vedaschi authored section 2.2; Chiara Graziani authored sections 1 and 2.1.

Chapter 6: Arianna Vedaschi authored sections 1.2 and 2.2; Chiara Graziani authored sections 1.1 and 2.1.

Chapter 7: Arianna Vedaschi authored section 2; Chiara Graziani authored section 1.

Part II Final Overview: This final overview is the result of shared thoughts of both authors.

Conclusions: The conclusions of this work are the result of shared thoughts between the two authors.

Introduction: the complex relationship between advanced technology, security and rights

As in every other aspect of everyday life, the field of national security is increasingly being affected by the pervasive use of technology, including artificial intelligence algorithms. Although the assumption that technology per se is a neutral tool – neither 'good' nor 'evil' – is particularly true in the field of security, the sensitive nature of security matters calls for close attention to be paid to the impact of these technologies on the legal protection of rights and freedoms and, ultimately, on the basic features of the rule of law.

The legal consequences of advanced technology on the rule of law can be assessed from two main angles: on one side, technology is a powerful tool *in the hands* of terrorists, being exploited by them and their organisations to serve their criminal purposes; on the other, it is an essential ally for public authorities – and for other actors cooperating with them – in *countering* the terrorist threat and *preventing* terrorist actions.

As far as the counter-terrorist use of technology is concerned, a further complicating factor comes into play, i.e., the balance between rights and freedoms, on the one hand, and security, on the other hand. In clearer words, when technology is massively used as a counter-terrorism tool, it might make the already challenging relationship between rights and security even more complex. As a matter of fact, technology becomes a 'third player', which often emphasises the side effects of national security measures, especially when rights such as privacy, data protection, and free speech are at stake; and even some basic principles of rule-of-law-based legal systems, such as non-discrimination and the presumption of innocence, might be put under stress.[1]

The critical and crucial issues brought by technology, both as a *terrorist tool* and as a *counter-terrorist* tool, even increase when the technology at hand is in its most advanced form available so far, that is, artificial intelligence algorithms. By artificial intelligence, we refer to systems that are autonomous and are able to mimic human reasoning (or at least parts or steps of it), thus having their own self-sufficient role in decision-making, not determined by any human operator.[2]

To understand correctly what is meant by 'artificial intelligence', we need to make a distinction between *autonomous* tools and *automated* ones. Starting from this second category, all technological instruments can be defined as automated because they carry out a certain task without human intervention. Let us think of a spreadsheet running the

1 Balkin refers to the idea of a triangle in this regard, analysing in particular the consequences on free speech. Jack M. Balkin, 'Free Speech is a Triangle' (2012) 118 Columbia LR 2011. On the first corner of the triangle, he places States or supranational organisations, striving to guarantee security; on the second corner, he puts internet infrastructure companies (hence, technology); and on the third and last angle, there are media, civil society organisations, and others reclaiming their right to free speech.

2 We take this definition of artificial intelligence with the awareness that there are voices according to which artificial intelligence can be defined as neither artificial nor intelligent. They argue that, in spite of their autonomy, these systems still draw from the work of real humans and do not 'invent' anything, differently from what human beings can do. Moreover, the type of intelligence they are endowed with is a 'pattern-matching' one, which is not the only kind of intelligence available to human beings. See Evgeny Morozov, 'The problem with artificial intelligence? It's neither artificial nor intelligent', *The Guardian*, 30 March 2023. According to Luciano Floridi, artificial intelligence is not autonomous, at least in 'creative' operations, since it always needs to rely on input data introduced by the human operator. In other words, they only show 'intelligent conduct'. Luciano Floridi, *Etica dell'intelligenza artificiale* (Cortina 2022); Id, 'L'intelligenza artificiale non ci ruberà il lavoro. E soprattutto non è intelligente,' Interview to *StartupItalia*, 25 June 2023 https://startupitalia.eu/startup/lintelligenza-artificiale-non-ci-rubera-il-lavoro-e-soprattutto-non-e-intelligente-parola-di-luciano-floridi/#:~:text=%C2%ABL'intelligenza%20artificiale%20non%20ci,Parola%20di%20Luciano%20Floridi%20%2D%20StartupItalia accessed 31 July 2024.

well-known Excel application: it is able to perform calculations millions of times more rapidly than the human mind would do; however, the spreadsheet is not autonomous because, at the end of its task, it comes to the very same conclusions that a human being performing the same calculations would have reached. Things are different with *autonomous* artificial intelligence. Being autonomous means that these technologies have the capacity to choose how to behave, based on a certain reasoning that they carry out, and this reasoning is not necessarily the same as that which a human being would have performed. The reasoning depends on data[3] 'feeding' the algorithm – which is, for sure, provided by a human operator through more or less complex programming procedures – but its conclusions (output) are autonomously determined by the algorithm itself. It is exactly on these autonomous systems that our book focuses, although some hints at more 'traditional' technologies are essential, both because such 'more ancient' technologies are still very popular as countermeasures in the comparative landscape and because they are sometimes 'merged' with intelligent algorithmic machines, thus creating 'updated versions' of traditional tools.

Examining the two mentioned sides (meaning the *terrorist* use of technology, especially artificial intelligence, and its *counter-terrorist* employment) in parallel is needed if one wants to get a full understanding of which are the bright and the dark sides of technology. With this in mind, we reflect on what law – i.e., legal regulation – can or cannot (and should or should not) do, what its potentialities and its limits are, and how it has to interact with entities different from traditional regulators (public authorities), such as internet platforms and the other so-called giants of technology or big techs. All of these are exactly the main aims, and so the research questions, of the present book, which we decided to write after several years of study and research into counter-terrorism measures and their evolution in the 'digital age'.[4] More precisely, we came to the deci-

---

[3] Often referred to as 'big data', designing well-working algorithms requires large amounts of data. For how algorithms are 'fed' with big data, see Robert Walters and Marko Nowak, *Cyber Security, Artificial Intelligence, Data Protection & The Law* (Springer 2021) 48.

[4] On the transformations brought in several fields by the digital age, see Tugrul U. Daim and Haydar Yalçın (eds), *Digital Transformations. New Tools and Methods for Mining Technological Intelligence* (Edward Elgar 2022); on the concept of 'digital', not just from the legal, but also from the

sion to write this book while carrying out a research project, funded by the Italian Ministry of Education and Research, on 'Decision-Making in the Age of Emergencies: New Paradigms in Recognition and Protection of Rights'. In pursuing the aim of such a research project – i.e., examining how the emergencies of the last twenty-five years (terrorism, financial turmoil, the pandemic, the resurgence of traditional war[5]) changed the classic paradigms and traditional decision-making processes – we identified a gap in legal[6] literature. Specifically, we realised that legal scholarly work is undoubtedly very developed regarding law and technology, and even richer in the field of national security measures, but it lacks a comprehensive work on law (meaning the guarantees for human rights and civil liberties), technology (specifically artificial intelligence), *and* national security, specifically counter-terrorism. In clearer and more detailed terms, scholars from all over the world have analysed in-depth the relationship between rights and security,[7] especially after 9/11 and the breakout of the international terrorist emergency. They have thought

---

philosophical and political science viewpoint, see, among others, Daniel Innerarity, 'European Digital Sovereignty' (2021) Institute of European Democrats Research Paper https://www.iedonline.eu/download/2021/IED-Research-Paper-Innerarity.pdf accessed 31 July 2024.

[5] In identifying recent emergencies, we decided not to mention other global crises, such as climate change and migration issues, since they can be defined as 'chronic' or at least 'cyclical' circumstances. In our view, they do not perfectly match the concept of emergency.

[6] As a matter of fact, many of the topics of this analysis are instead addressed by publications pertaining to other sciences, such as sociology, communication science, political science, and sometimes computer science. The legal perspective is instead still widely lacking. For this reason, many of the sources cited in this book are from other sciences, rather than purely legal ones.

[7] Giving an exhaustive list of literature on this topic would be too long and out of the scope of this book. Some of the most updated analyses on counter-terrorism in general can be found in the following works: Simon Frankel Pratt, *Normative Transformation and the War on Terrorism* (CUP 2023); Lara A. Frumkin, John F. Morrison and Andrew Silke (eds), *A Research Agenda for Terrorism Studies* (Edward Elgar 2023); Fiona de Londras, *Practice and Problems of Transnational Counter-Terrorism* (CUP 2022); Arianna Vedaschi and Kim Lane Scheppele (eds), *9/11 and Global Anti-Terrorism Law: How the UN Security Council Rules the World* (CUP 2021).

over the use of technology in general as a counter-terrorism tool and the legal issues it poses,[8] they have written a lot of useful works about cutting-edge artificial intelligence tools and their applications as well;[9] however, no in-depth piece has been delivered yet on this 'triangulation': technology (artificial intelligence), security (counter-terrorism), and rights. This is where we want to position our analysis, so giving rise to a new and specialised field of research.

In trying to fill this gap, the reason why we chose to focus on artificial intelligence rather than on any other kind of technology is that 'intelligent algorithms' represent the very latest frontier of technology. As a consequence, having a deep understanding of how they can be used in national security practice is crucial for anyone who wants to study any of these topics (the protection of rights, counter-terrorism, law, and technology). Moreover, we conceived this book as an updated tool that takes stock of the latest developments, so intelligent algorithms could not be left behind.

Another important caveat that we need to make in introducing our analysis is that we mainly focused on *international* terrorism, which refers to form of terrorism inspired by and grounded in jihadist extremist doctrines; nonetheless, many of the technological techniques that we examine are used both to spread and fight other types of terrorism, most notably domestic terrorism, whose resurgence in recent years is very well-known.[10]

---

[8] See, e.g., among the most recent works: Stuart Casey-Maslen, *International Counter-Terrorism Law* (CUP 2024); Ulrike Felt and Alan Irwing (eds), *Elgar Encyclopaedia of Science and Technology Studies* (Edward Elgar 2024) 553; David Gray and Stephen E. Henderson (eds), *The Cambridge Handbook of Surveillance Law* (CUP 2017) 5.

[9] Also in this regard, giving a complete account would not be feasible. We limit references to some of the most recent works: Alberto Quintavalla and Jeroen Temperman (eds), *Artificial Intelligence and Human Rights* (OUP 2023); Larry A. Di Matteo, Cristina Poncibò and Michel Cannarsa (eds), *The Cambridge Handbook of Artificial Intelligence. Global Perspectives on Law and Ethics* (CUP 2022); Simon Chesterman, *We, the Robots? Regulating Artificial Intelligence and the Limits of the Law* (OUP 2021).

[10] Several recent reports confirm this tendency: Institute for Economics and Peace, Global Terrorism Index 2024, February 2024 https://www.visionofhumanity.org/wp-content/uploads/2024/02/GTI-2024-web-290224.pdf accessed 31 July 2024; Europol, TE-SAT: European Union Terrorism

From the structural viewpoint, coherently with the abovementioned division between *terrorist* and *counter-terrorist* uses of technology, we envisaged two parts of this book, each dedicated to one of the two sides of the coin respectively. Part I is focused on technology as a terrorist weapon, i.e., it surveys how technology is instrumental in planning and executing terrorist strategies and actions, from radicalisation efforts to actual attacks. Part II is centred on counter-terrorism measures relying on advanced technologies, i.e., the technologies enhancing action by law enforcement and intelligence bodies, struggling against the terrorist threat. At first sight, these two different perspectives could seem opposite; instead, they show a strong interplay, since the policy and legal responses (examined in Part II) cannot be framed without knowing how the threat (i.e., terrorist cells or groups) exploits the same technologies (which is the core of Part I). More in detail, if law enforcement authorities, intelligence services, and other bodies working in counter-terrorism do not know how terrorists exploit technology, they will never be able to frame – often in partnership with private bodies – a set of well-working and effective counter-measures, as a 'competitive advantage' would be left to the terrorists themselves. Additionally, and this is a further yet essential complicating factor, they need to apply these technologies in a way that is compatible with basic principles of the rule of law, in order not to renounce the 'DNA' of advanced democracies.

From a methodological viewpoint, as comparative law scholars, we embrace in our book a comparative methodology and chose to mainly take into account major Western advanced democracies. By Western advanced democracies, we mean countries of Western Europe grounded in the liberal tradition as well as North American ones (especially the United States, but some references to Canada are made, too, when relevant). When analysing the European legal environment, we decided to pay particular attention to the consequences of Brexit in terms of security and from the angle of technology. As a matter of fact, the decision of the United Kingdom to leave the European Union, besides being a

Situation and Trend Report 2023, 19 December 2023 https://www.europol.europa.eu/publication-events/main-reports/european-union-terrorism-situation-and-trend-report-2023-te-sat#downloads accessed 31 July 2024; US Department of State, Country Reports on Terrorism 2022, 30 November 2023 https://www.state.gov/wp-content/uploads/2023/11/Country_Reports_on_Terrorism_2022-v3.pdf accessed 31 July 2024.

unique case study – since, so far, no further Member States have activated Article 50 of the Treaty on the European Union (TEU)[11] – spread interest from our perspective for two main reasons. The first reason is that the United Kingdom has always been a top player in European security policies, being the 'link' between the European Union and the 'Five Eyes alliance'.[12] Thus, the fact that it became a 'third country' in EU law, due to Brexit, triggered the need to find tailor-made solutions aimed at not weakening its essential contribution in the field of intelligence and, hence, security safeguards. The second reason for focussing on Brexit in certain passages of this book is that, after the transition period,[13] the United Kingdom is no longer bound to apply the law of the European Union nor to implement it in its legal system. Consequently, it is coming up with its own solutions that sometimes align to what Member States are doing, while in other cases show significant differences. This phenomenon is very interesting to analyse through the lenses of comparative

---

[11] Article 50 TEU is the provision containing the procedure to be followed by Member States to leave the European Union if they decide to do so based on their constitutional norms. For a discussion of this norm, also in relation to the well-known case of *R (Miller) v Secretary of State for Exiting the European Union* [2017] UKSC 5, see Piet Eeckhout and Eleni Frantziou, 'Brexit and Article 50 TEU: A Constitutionalist Reading' (2017) 54 CMLR 695.

[12] The Five Eyes alliance is a network established at the end of the Second World War, comprising the main common law countries, i.e., Australia, Canada, New Zealand, the United Kingdom, and the United States, aimed at sharing intelligence information and cooperating in this field. Their work has the purpose of fighting the main national security threats and safeguarding global security. Paul F. Scott, *National Security Constitutionalism in the Commonwealth Five Eyes States* (Hart Publishing, forthcoming); Anthony R. Wells, *Between Five Eyes: 50 Years of Intelligence Sharing* (Casemate 2020); Zachary K. Goldman and Samuel J. Rascoff (eds), *Global Intelligence Oversight: Governing Security in the Twenty-First Century* (OUP 2016).

[13] In the context of the Brexit negotiations, the transition period was that time span ranging from the day on which the United Kingdom formally left the European Union (31 January 2020) to the signature of the agreement on the future relationships between the two parties (24 December 2020). Federico Fabbrini (ed), *The New Framework of New EU-UK Relations* (OUP 2021).

law scholars and with regard to its impact on the relationship between technology and security.

Along with the mentioned countries, all geographically belonging to Europe (if not legally to the European Union) or to North America, throughout our manuscript we often take into consideration, when necessary, two countries that are not physically part of the Western world, but that can easily be introduced in the comparative effort due to similar cultural, historical, and legal environments with Western democracies, especially the United Kingdom. Reference is to Australia and New Zealand, which frequently provide crucial food for thought for our work.

Once we have set this comparative environment, i.e., the countries targeted by our analysis, we need to clarify that, in the progress of our study in this book, we do not always examine each and every of the mentioned legal contexts; in fact, we chose to rely on the so-called prototypical case logic,[14] meaning that for each topic, we bring out the legal system(s) among the ones methodologically selected, where the specific measure and/or issues have been mainly observed and trigger more interesting considerations.

Moreover, the perspective of 'vertical comparison' is not left aside in this book, in the awareness that domestic measures are often the result of a complex multilevel governmental interplay, and this is especially true in this field, being that terrorism is a 'global' threat.[15] As a consequence, the international and supranational dimensions are addressed when relevant. In this regard, European Union legislation and policy play a crucial role, especially over the last ten years, along with and more than those actors belonging to 'universal international law' – most of all the United Nations and derived bodies – who laid down their guidelines, which we examine in due course throughout our work.

Last but not least, and still from a methodological point of view, it needs to be highlighted that the topic we address is characterised by a strong interdisciplinary approach. In effect, both from the side of the terrorist use of technology and the counter-terrorist employments, a full understanding of the issue implies the interaction of law, computer sciences, and even psychological, sociological, and behavioral studies. In this book, we point out these interactions when necessary and, although

---

[14] Ran Hirschl, 'The Question of Case Selection in Comparative Law' (2005) 53 AJCL 125.

[15] Arianna Vedaschi and Kim Lane Scheppele (eds), *op. cit.*

our perspective is the legal one, we give a picture of the complexity caused by the connections of several sciences.

Lastly, since this volume is conceived for a very wide audience – from scholars, to students, to practitioners – we intend our book both as a theoretical scholarly analysis and as a practical tool, and we introduce several graphs and tables throughout the manuscript, in the hope that they will facilitate our readers to better grasp the main challenges posed by technology in times of terrorism.

PART I

Technology as a 'terrorist tool'

A general overview: the intersection between technology and terrorist activities

Terrorism, both in its domestic and international forms, runs through the web and, more specifically, through advanced technologies. Plenty of data is available to prove this statement. Just to mention some national statistics, a 2021 report requested by the UK House of Commons[1] about the prevalent sources and mechanisms of radicalisation among individuals convicted of terrorist, extremist, or extremist-related offences in England and Wales demonstrated that, from 2005 to 2017, the number of those who radicalised through the internet increased sharply, considering both individuals who radicalised exclusively online and others who radicalised due to the combined action of online and offline sources.[2] At the same time, the influence of offline radicalisation (including face-to-face contact with extremists) considerably decreased.[3] This trend was confirmed one year later by a further study commissioned by the UK Ministry of Justice,[4] where researchers found that, from 2017 to 2019,

[1] Jonathan Kenyon and Jens Binder, 'Christopher Baker-Beall, Exploring the Role of the Internet in Radicalisation and Offending of Convicted Extremists', HM Prison and Probation Service, Ministry of Justice Analytical Series (2021) https://assets.publishing.service.gov.uk/media/614088c2e90e070442fbdde2/exploring-role-internet-radicalisation.pdf accessed 31 July 2024.

[2] To give detailed percentages: 83% in 2015–2017, 64% in 2010–2014, 35% in 2005–2009.

[3] More in detail, reported percentages are: 17% in 2015–2017, 36% in 2010–2014, and 65% in 2005–2009.

[4] Jonathan Kenyon, Jens Binder and Christopher Baker-Beall, 'The Internet and Radicalisation Pathways: Technological Advances, Relevance of Mental Health, and Role of Attackers', HM Prison and Probation Service, Ministry of Justice Analytical Series (2022) https://assets.publishing.service

online and 'hybrid' (meaning a mixture of offline and online) radicalisation had even risen to 92%. Therefore, only the remaining 8% occurs totally offline. Other recent inquiries, conducted by psychologists and social scientists and published in sectorial journals, confirm this overall tendency, giving evidence of the prevalence of online radicalisation in the current scenario.[5]

Besides being used as a hotspot for radicalisation, attracting potential adepts, the internet is also resorted to in order to materially plan and prepare terrorist actions. If one looks at data regarding perpetrators of completed or thwarted jihadist attacks, reported most recently in 2022 by the Global Network on Extremism and Technology[6] and showing that a high percentage of attackers planned their crimes online, the role of the internet as a place to discuss and organise forthcoming attacks emerges patently.[7] For instance, there is evidence that the 2015 Paris attacks were organised using Twitter (the current name of which is X).[8] The same can be said regarding some attacks which took place in the Middle East.[9]

Notably, some studies conducted by the United Nations Security Council Counter-Terrorism Executive Directorate (UNCTED) point out that terrorists' reliance on the internet to carry out their activities (from indoctrination to the actual arrangement of attacks) was boosted by the breakout of the Covid-19 pandemic in 2020 and its several waves that

---

.gov.uk/media/638f089bd3bf7f327e1ea969/internet-radicalisation-report.pdf accessed 31 July 2024.

[5] Jens F. Binder and Jonathan Kenyon, 'Terrorism and the Internet: How Dangerous is Online Radicalisation?' (2022) 13 Forensic and Legal Psychology 1.

[6] Nafees Hamid and Cristina Ariza, 'Offline Versus Online Radicalisation: Which is the Bigger Threat? Tracing Outcomes of 439 Jihadist Terrorists Between 2014–2021' (2022) 8 Western Countries, Report of the Global Network on Extremism and Technology https://gnet-research.org/wp-content/uploads/2022/02/GNET-Report-Offline-Versus-Online-Radicalisation.pdf accessed 31 July 2024.

[7] Such a percentage amounts to 46%.

[8] Pooja N. Jain and Archana S. Vaidaya, 'Analysis of Social Media Based on Terrorism – A Review' (2021) 8 Vietnam Journal of Computer Science 8.

[9] Istituto per gli Studi di Politica Internazionale (ISPI), 'The Roots and Ramifications of Terrorism in Iran', 26 February 2024 https://www.ispionline.it/en/publication/the-roots-and-ramifications-of-terrorism-in-iran-165017.

raged through 2021 and 2022.[10] This trend, highlighted by the UNCTED, toward the digitalisation of terrorist activities is coherent with the general rise in the use of technology by civil society that was fueled, among other factors, by the recent pandemic. After all, since digital tools are increasingly an essential part of the life of each and every individual, the spread of technology has inevitably affected criminal activities and, in particular, terrorist ones.

From their own criminal perspective, terrorists gain several advantages from moving (wholly or partially) their activities from the offline to the online dimension. To synthesise these advantages, we can mention at least four main beneficial aspects from the viewpoint of terrorists. The first benefit is the broadness of the audience, since disseminating any content through online resources allows radicalisers to reach virtually any corner of the world, connecting people without any effort. Moreover, and here are the second and third benefits, the quickness and very low costs guaranteed by the use of the internet are unprecedented. The fourth advantage for terrorists is secrecy that at least some types of technology ensure: let us think, e.g., of encrypted instant messaging apps but also of the deepest 'layers' of the web, namely the dark web, which is able to provide terrorists with almost inviolable 'safe heavens'.[11] All these factors together urged terrorists to move several of their activities online.

In addition, it has to be borne in mind that, while the abovementioned advantages are common to any kind of technology (even the relatively 'oldest' ones), most recent and advanced tools, often based on artificial intelligence (AI), may offer further, attractive benefits to terrorists and extremists. As highlighted in 2021 by the United Nations Office for

[10] United Nations Security Council Counter-Terrorism Committee Executive Directorate, 'The Impact of the COVID-19 Pandemic on Terrorism, Counter-terrorism and Countering Violent Extremism' (December 2021) https://www.un.org/securitycouncil/ctc/sites/www.un.org.securitycouncil.ctc/files/files/documents/2021/Dec/cted_covid19_paper_dec_2021.pdf accessed 31 July 2024.

[11] Gabriel Weimann, 'Terrorist Migration on the Dark Web' (2016) 10 Perspectives on Terrorism 40; Beatrice Berton, 'The Dark Side of the Web: ISIL's One-stop Shop?, Report of the European Union Institute for Security Studies', June 2015 https://www.files.ethz.ch/isn/192064/Alert_30_The_Dark_Web.pdf accessed 31 July 2024.

Counter-Terrorism,[12] intelligent algorithms can be maliciously used to enhance terrorist decision-making by replacing (efficiently, from the terrorists' viewpoint) their offline efforts in identifying targets, gathering relevant elements to carry out cyber-attacks, and several other actions that will be addressed ahead in the present analysis.

Given that an inextricable – and progressively tightening – relationship exists between technology and terrorist activities, this part of our book builds a taxonomy of possible ways of using advanced tools from the side of terrorists. This is essential, not only for mere classification purposes but also to help those who design counter-terrorism measures (policymakers, lawmakers, non-governmental and private bodies cooperating with them) to be aware of what they have to face and how they can respond.

In our effort to classify the terrorist exploitation of technology, a pivotal initial distinction should be made between terrorist activities carried out through digital tools in the *real* digital world and those activities performed (or that might be performed) in the so-called metaverse. This distinction is peculiar and deserves some more words. In this book, by 'real digital world' we mean the 'traditional' digital activities, i.e., those that are performed virtually and still have an impact on reality. Let us think, by way of example, of posting some content (a message, a photo, a video, etc.) on a social media. The content is posted in a digital space, and the digital message exists in the real world. The metaverse, instead, is something different, since it consists of an 'augmented' reality, able to generate a new environment, replicating, but not coinciding with, the real one. More precisely, the metaverse has been defined as 'a virtual world where humans, as avatars, interact with each other in a three-dimensional space that *mimics* reality',[13] and it is the latest breakthrough of technology advancement. Nowadays, the metaverse is still in the very initial

---

[12] United Nations Office for Counter-Terrorism, UN Counter-Terrorism Centre (CTC), 'Algorithms and Terrorism: The Malicious Use of Artificial Intelligence for Terrorist Purposes' (2021) https://www.un.org/counterterrorism/sites/www.un.org.counterterrorism/files/malicious-use-of-ai-uncct-unicri-report-hd.pdf accessed 31 July 2024.

[13] Definition provided by the Cambridge Dictionary of 'Metaverse' https://dictionary.cambridge.org/it/dizionario/inglese/metaverse accessed 31 July 2024 (emphasis added).

stage of its development; however, it has a potential dark side that, based on recent studies,[14] is very likely to be exploited by terrorists. In order to better outline the taxonomy that we set out and will develop *infra*, we decided to provide the readers with an Appendix to Part I, which gives a more schematic framework of this categorisation.

[14] Joel S. Elson, Austin C. Doctor and Sam Hunter, 'The Metaverse Offers a Future Full of Potential – For Terrorists and Extremists, Too', *The Conversation*, 7 January 2022 https://theconversation.com/the-metaverse-offers-a-future-full-of-potential-for-terrorists-and-extremists-too-173622 accessed 31 July 2024; Suraj Lakhani, Jessica White and Claudia Wallner, 'The Gamification of (Violent) Extremism. An Exploration of Emerging Trends, Future Threats Scenarios and Potential P/CVE Solutions', European Commission, Radicalisation Awareness Network Policy Support (2022) https://home-affairs.ec.europa.eu/system/files/2022-09/RAN%20Policy%20Support-%20gamification%20of%20violent%20extremism_en.pdf accessed 31 July 2024.

1. The use of technology in terrorist activities in the 'real digital world'

Starting from applications of technology for terrorist purposes in what we called the 'real digital world',[1] a couple of preliminary caveats need to be highlighted.

First, in the effort to systematise the possible ways in which technology is used to serve the criminal aims of terrorists, we have considered different stages of involvement in terrorist activities: from terrorist groups' endeavors to attract other people and urge them to embrace terrorist ideologies, to the preparation of acts, the training of adepts, and up to incitement or the actual commission of terrorist attacks. In doing so, we have to refer to some concepts, such as 'propaganda', 'glorification', 'apology', and 'incitement' of terrorist acts, in a necessarily a-technical way, that is, without contextualising these words in any specific domestic criminal system. These expressions may indeed take partially different meanings based on different legal contexts,[2] but it would not be useful for the purpose of the current classification to differentiate in detail their significance in each legal system. Consequently, we decided to consider 'incitement' in the meaning that is most frequently given to it in the comparative scenario, i.e., directly and explicitly pushing someone to

1 As stated, for the purposes of this analysis, by 'real digital world', we mean all those manifestations of the digital environment that differ from the metaverse (i.e., 'ordinary' digital tools).

2 For an explanation of how different terms are used in different legal contexts, see Arianna Vedaschi, 'Humiliation of Terrorism Victims: Is Human Dignity Becoming a '"National Security Tool"?', in Christophe Paulussen and Martin Scheinin (eds), *Human Dignity and Human Security in Times of Terrorism* (Springer 2020) 299; Helen Duffy and Kate Pitcher, 'Inciting Terrorism? Crimes of Expression and the Limits of the Law', Grotius Centre Working Papers Series No. 2018/076-HRL – 4 April 2018 https://papers.ssrn.com/sol3/papers.cfm?abstract_id=3156210 accessed 31 July 2024.

commit a terrorist act or to embrace the terrorist ideology; and we intend other terms, such as 'apology', 'glorification', 'propaganda', and similar ones as indirect and implicit encouragement, consisting, e.g., of praising terrorist acts or terrorist ideas, acclaiming extremist doctrines, spreading glory on past terrorist attacks, and other forms of non-explicit but still potentially dangerous behaviors.[3] No doubt all of these types of conduct can be qualified as attempts at radicalisation, i.e., efforts to have other 'adepts' embrace terrorist ideas, eventually – even if not necessarily – leading to the commission of acts. Therefore, with these radicalising conducts, we are at a stage that is preliminary to full-fledged recruitment, as they consist of terrorists (already radicalised) trying to convince other people.

The second preliminary caveat is that, in our taxonomy, we found it useful to make a distinction between the use of the 'surface web' and that of the 'dark web' by terrorists. As known, the web can be conceived as a very wide platform composed of several layers:[4] from the 'surface' layers (so-called surface web), which can be accessed by standard search engines, to some 'deeper' layers, which are neither accessible nor even indexed by traditional search engines (like Google, Safari, etc.). Among 'deeper' layers (so-called deep web), some contain illegal content,[5] voluntarily concealed by their authors. These illegal features are normally found in the so-called dark web, i.e., a sub-category of the deep web containing websites whose IP address is concealed (see Figure 1.1 and Figure 1.2). The privacy or rather anonymity or, in general, lack of transparency guaranteed by the dark web makes it a virtual place highly exploited by terrorists. On the dark web, it is possible to spread information that, if disseminated through 'surface' channels, would be immediately labelled as criminal and undoubtedly prosecuted as such by law enforcement authorities.[6]

---

[3] Olivier Roy, *Jihad and Death. The Global Appeal of the Islamic State* (Hurst 2017).

[4] Babak Akhgar, Marco Gercke, Stefanos Vrochidis and Helen Gibson (eds), *Dark Web Investigation* (Springer 2021); Gabriel Weimann, 'Going Dark: Terrorism on the Dark Web' (2016) 39 Studies in Conflict & Terrorism 195.

[5] It is worth highlighting, however, that not all of the contents of the deep web are illegal. The deep web can host, among others, content related to trade secrets or investigative journalism.

[6] For instance, explicit and direct incitement, or instructions to carry out an attack.

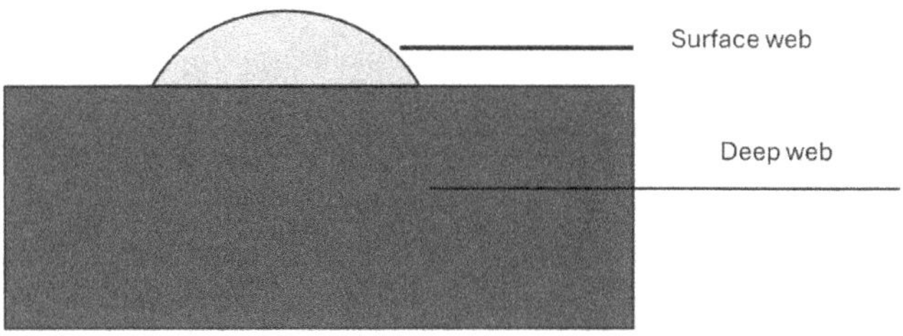

Source: Authors.

Figure 1.1 *The levels of the web*

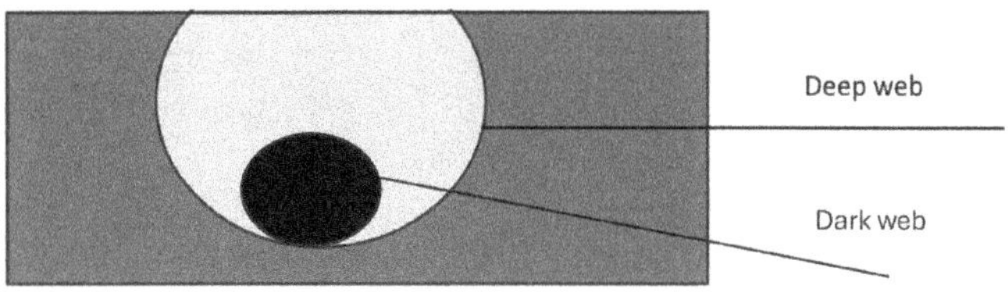

Source: Authors.

Figure 1.2 *The dark web*

Given this differentiation between surface and (deep and most of all) dark web, sections 1, 2 and 3 are focused on terrorist activities that are mainly carried out through the surface web, while section 4 is wholly dedicated to the dark web.

1. INDOCTRINATION ATTEMPTS ON THE WEB

As clarified before, there are several methods that terrorists use in order to attract, directly or indirectly, other people into their ideology, with the aim of recruiting them to become a part of an organised 'army' of jihadist extremists. Such an 'army' can ultimately be identified as a group of 'citizens', satisfying terrorists' 'state-like' ambitions, well-demonstrated throughout time. For this reason, these adepts are often defined, among others, as the 'citizenry' or the 'people' of terrorism.[7] Although these types of recruiting and radicalising behavior can be carried out both offline and online, the digital environment offers plenty of opportunities for terrorists to boost their efforts and broaden the reach of their message, thanks to the reset of the spatial and temporal dimensions that the web allows. As a consequence, as soon as the internet became widespread and available to most people in their everyday life without significant costs, terrorists promptly converted their offline radicalisation strategies into online tactics, exploiting the digital dimension.[8] When these activities are deployed on the surface (and not in the dark) web, they do not consist, normally, of direct incitement or explicit instructions given regarding how to commit a terrorist act – something that would be immediately identified by public authorities and prosecuted accordingly, so it would not be convenient for terrorists to behave like that. Rather, when they act on 'superficial' layers of the web, rather than on the 'dark web', terrorists rely on more 'nuanced' patterns, such as glorification, apology, and other forms of 'softer' indoctrination.

In this regard, the main strategies resort to the use of three distinct groups of tools: first, social media (and other platforms that can be assimilated to them); second, chat rooms; third, instant messaging services.

Social media can be defined as 'websites and computer programmes that allow people to communicate and share information *on* the Internet'.[9] A chatroom is a 'virtual channel where users communicate with each other *through* the Internet'.[10] Instant messaging services, instead, are

---

[7] Arianna Vedaschi, 'Da al-Qāʿida all'IS: il terrorismo internazionale si è fatto Stato?' (2016) 66 Rivista trimestrale di diritto pubblico 41.

[8] Among the several studies carried out by experts in sociology and communication, see Philip Baugut and Katharina Neumann, 'Online Propaganda Use during Islamist Radicalisation' (2023) 23 Information, Communication & Society 1570; Paul Baines, Nancy Snow, and Nicholas O'Shaughnessy (eds), *The SAGE Handbook of Propaganda* (SAGE 2019).

[9] The Cambridge Dictionary, 'Social media' https://dictionary.cambridge.org/dictionary/english/social-media accessed 31 July 2024. Emphasis added.

[10] The Cambridge Dictionary, 'Chatroom' https://www.techopedia.com/definition/389/chat-room accessed 31 July 2024. Emphasis added.

tools allowing 'the exchange of near-real-time messages through a standalone application or embedded software'.[11]

The difference between social media and the other two tools is quite evident. In fact, a post (written text, image, video, audio) uploaded on social media can be abstractly accessed by any user who has an account,[12] while instant messaging services[13] and chatrooms imply an exchange of communication between identified (or at least identifiable) users. In other words, social media messages are *on* the internet, while those exchanged through chatrooms and instant messaging services run *through* the internet.

That being said, there is also a difference between chatrooms and instant messaging services. Such divergence lies in the fact that, unlike a chatroom, instant messaging services are normally used for conversations following the one-to-one model or addressing (relatively) limited groups of identified or identifiable participants; while chatrooms usually allow a dialogue among large amounts of people who are interested in the same topic and are normally admitted to join the chatroom by one or more moderators. This distinction has actually been partially overcome insofar as some instant messaging services – such as WhatsApp or Telegram[14] – have established 'channels', which can be subscribed to by individual users and replicate the functioning of a chatroom, with the further advantage that, while chatrooms are built to be used through computers, these channels are normally smartphone and tablet-friendly, so they can be easily managed through portable devices. Moreover,

---

[11] The Cambridge Dictionary, 'Instant Messaging' https://www.techtarget.com/searchunifiedcommunications/definition/instant-messaging accessed 31 July 2024.

[12] For an analysis, Katherine E. Brown and Elizabeth Pearson, 'Social media, the online environment and terrorism', in Andrew Silke (ed), *Routledge Handbook of Terrorism and Counterterrorism* (Routledge 2018) 47.

[13] Megan Thomas-Evans, 'The Internet, Social Media and the Internet of Things in Radicalisation to Terrorism and Violent Extremism', in Reza Montasari, Fiona Carroll, Ian Mitchell, Sukhvinder Hara and Rachel Bolton-King (eds), *Privacy, Security And Forensics in The Internet of Things (IoT)'*(Springer 2022) 179.

[14] Miron Lakomy, 'Mapping Digital Jihad: Understanding the Structure and Evolution of al-Qaeda's Information Ecosystem on the Surface Web' (2024) 18 Perspectives on Terrorism 82.

WhatsApp and Telegram channels – unlike 'ordinary' chatrooms – can count on end-to-end encryption, something that can be highly advantageous when illegal activities are carried out (see *infra*).

Focussing on terrorists' use of social media, available studies[15] show that terrorists primarily use Facebook (Meta), Twitter (now X), and YouTube. It appears that terrorists prefer to resort to these platforms due to their features enabling users to rapidly upload and share materials as well as react extremely quickly to content posted by others. Consequently, terrorists can easily disseminate their propaganda, often in the form of posts, audio-videos, or images. Some studies demonstrated that terrorist communication on social media is structured and organised as a sort of pyramid,[16] with central leaders at its top who identify the topics for media communication, immediately followed by other members of the group who have the role of 'media managers' and concretely post and handle the online content. At the bottom of the pyramid, there are all virtual supporters, who visualise and share the content, creating a sort of chain. As far as the type of content is concerned, scholars highlighted that terrorist propaganda is often concealed behind titles that appear to have nothing to do with extremism.[17] For instance, an extremist video can be hidden behind a title and cover page referring to the ordinary use of weapons; this strategy is especially successful in countries such as the United States, where carrying weapons is considered lawful, and many users can be interested in such content.

Regarding the use of chatrooms by terrorists, even if it has slightly decreased in recent years – due to the shift to social media,[18] which indeed often incorporate chatroom services – it is still a very common way to spread terrorist propaganda. Chatrooms offer an advantage, i.e.,

---

[15] Sara Zeiger and Joseph Gyte, 'Prevention of Radicalisation on Social Media and the Internet', in Alex P. Schmid (ed), *Handbook of Terrorism Prevention and Preparedness* (ICCT Press 2021) 358; Gabriel Weimann, 'Terrorist Migration to Social Media' (2015) 16 Georgetown J Intl Aff 180.

[16] Phillip Seib and Dana M. Janbek, *Global Terrorism and New Media: The Post-Al Qaeda Generation* (Routledge 2011).

[17] Yael Stein, 'Social Networks – Terrorism's New Marketplace' (2011) Genocide Prevention Now 7.

[18] On the new digital environment for terrorist radicalization, see Gary A. Ackerman, 'The Emerging Terrorist Technological Landscape', in Nicholas Stockhammer (ed), *Routledge Handbook of Transnational Terrorism* (Routledge 2024) 97.

they gather groups of people interested in the same topic and allow them to easily interact. For example, it has been reported[19] that radicalised people often share their personal experiences in fighting for terrorism or praise the 'martyrdom' of terrorists, in an attempt to involve others. Like content on social media, these chatrooms, not being located in the 'darker' part of the web, often need to be disguised, e.g., in the form of religious or charity groups,[20] and normally do not contain explicit instructions on how to engage in terrorist acts (something that, instead, characterises dark web tools, on which see *infra*).

Shifting to the terrorist use of instant messaging services, these are probably the most popular and user-friendly technology in everyday life, so terrorists did not hesitate to strive in order to spread their messages even through them. As hinted above, one of the biggest advantages provided to terrorists by these applications is the so-called end-to-end encryption.[21] End-to-end encryption is a method invented primarily to protect users' privacy and personal data. In practice, this type of encryption ensures that data exchanged through instant messaging services is not accessible by third parties, and not even by the owners of the service itself (e.g., WhatsApp). In other words, messages and, in general, content exchanged through these technologies can only be decrypted by the recipient's device and cannot be accessed by any other device. While this method undoubtedly serves the purpose of guaranteeing users' privacy, at the same time it hinders public authorities' ability to intercept communication and carry out surveillance (although, as will be clarified in Part II, some measures have been developed in order to access this type of encrypted data).[22] In light of the undeniable benefits offered by encryption in terms of privacy and secrecy of communications, terrorists use

---

[19] Gabriel Weimann, 'Terror on Facebook, Twitter, and YouTube' (2010) 16 The Brown Journal of World Affairs 45.

[20] Des Freedman and Daya Thussu, *War and the Media: Reporting Conflict 24/7* (Sage 2003).

[21] Robert E. Endeley, 'End-to-End Encryption in Messaging Services and National Security – Case of WhatsApp Messenger' (2018) 9 Journal of Information Security 95.

[22] For some examples focused on a specific jurisdiction, Nicola McGarrity and Keiran Hardy, 'Digital Surveillance and Access to Encrypted Communications in Australia' (2020) 49 Common Law World Review 160.

these encrypted apps for multiple aims.[23] First, to share news regarding the Islamic State's actions and its military successes, especially in territories like Iraq or Central and Western Africa. Second, they resort to these platforms to share links to material posted on cloud-sharing apps (such as Dropbox, OneDrive, 4Share, etc.).[24] Since owners of cloud-sharing platforms – which are not encrypted – may remove these contents, terrorists often continuously upload identical materials on a variety of platforms, so as to ensure that they are never completely removed. Third, terrorists resort to instant messaging apps even to share links of so-called terrorist databases. The latter are organised collections of publications, such as magazines, books, pamphlets, and advertising messages, that disseminate the terrorist ideology. These publications, which can be referred to as the 'terrorist press', are the focus of the following section.

2. THE 'TERRORIST PRESS': THE DISSEMINATION OF ONLINE TERRORIST MAGAZINES

Even before 2014 – when the Islamic State self-proclaimed as a State[25] – several publications conveying terrorist ideas and methods had already been issued.[26] Most of them are still present online and are disseminated through the methods addressed above, as one of the several radicalisation techniques.

The first online magazine was launched by Al-Qaeda in 2003 and was called Sawt al-Jihad (in Arabic, Voice of Jihad).[27] After it was shut down in 2005 by Saudi security services, a plethora of other magazines started to be published in several languages (not just in Arabic and English, but

---

[23] Gabriel Weimann and Asia Vellante, 'The Dead Drops of Online Terrorism' (2021) Perspectives on Terrorism 15, 39.

[24] Victoria A. Correia and Moufida Sadok, 'Governing Online Terrorist Propaganda: A Societal Security Issue', Proceedings of the 7th International Workshop on Socio-Technical Perspective in IS development (STPIS 2021).

[25] Arianna Vedaschi, 'Da al-Qāʿida all'IS: il terrorismo internazionale si è fatto Stato?, *op. cit.*

[26] Robert J. Bunker and Pamela Bunnker, *Radical Islamist English-Language Online Magazines: Research Guide, Strategic Insights, and Policy Response* (US Army War College Press 2018).

[27] Thomas Hegghammer, *Jihadi Culture* (CUP 2017) 226.

even in French, German, Russian, and Turkish). Their fates have been varied: some of them have been closed relatively early after their inception due to varying reasons, including lack of audience, capture or death of their initiators or editors, or changes in the structure of the group that gave rise to them; others have instead survived for a longer time before being dismissed based on public authorities' orders.

Among the most well-known and enduring magazines are Inspire, founded by Al-Qaeda in 2010 and still active, and Dabiq,[28] named after a town located in Northern Syria, which was run by the Islamic State from 2014 to 2016. Dabiq was later renamed Rumiyah and expired in 2017.[29]

Inspire's original editors were Samir Khan and Sheik Anwar al-Awlaki, who were both killed in September 2011 in a drone strike in Yemen supervised by the United States through the Central Intelligence Agency (CIA). After some time, the two editors were replaced by Yahya Ibrahim. The main content of Inspire consists of 'Open Source Jihad',[30] a section aimed at promoting 'lone-wolf' attacks carried out through ordinary items, and explanations on how to use available technologies to radicalise others. Additionally, this magazine has often given voice to well-known figures of jihadist extremism through 'letters to the editor'.[31]

Dabiq was founded in 2014, coinciding with the Islamic State's self-proclamation, and it was unmistakably one of the tools used to promote state-like aspirations of terrorists. Relationships with the press and the media in general are something that strongly characterises State entities and helps them maintain their trust relationships with their citizens. The main purpose of Dabiq was to encourage Western recruits to migrate to the territories owned by the Caliphate, thus enhancing the phenomenon of foreign terrorist fighters,[32] particularly widespread in those years.

---

[28] Haroro J. Ingram, 'An Analysis of Inspire and Dabiq: Lessons from AQAP and Islamic State's Propaganda War' (2016) 40 Studies in Conflict & Terrorism 357.

[29] Mirom Lakomy, 'Recruitment and Incitement to Violence in the Islamic State's Online Propaganda: Comparative Analysis of Dabiq and Rumiyah' (2021) Studies in Conflicts & Terrorism 44.

[30] Per-Erik Nilsson, *Open Source Jihad: Problematising the Academic Discourse on Islamic Terrorism in Contemporary Europe* (CUP 2018).

[31] Robert J. Bunker, Pamela Bunnker, *op. cit.*, 13.

[32] On the foreign terrorist fighters' phenomenon, Andrea de Guttry, Francesca Capone, and Christophe Paulussen (eds), *Foreign Terrorist Fighters under International Law* (Asser Press 2016); Alex P. Schmid and

Unlike Inspire, Dabiq did not have any identified editors, and the authors of all contributions were anonymous. With the decline of the Islamic State and the loss of its territories in 2016, Dabiq came to an end and was quickly replaced by Rumiyah. Rumiyah is the Arabic name of the city of Rome, so the magazine was a way to allude to the fall and reconstruction of that city in the past. It has been observed[33] that, compared to Dabiq, Rumiyah relies on a different narrative. In particular, rather than encouraging foreign terrorist fighters to move from the Western world to the territories of the Islamic State (which, meanwhile, had been lost), the articles which appeared on the magazine urged people to carry out jihad wherever they were located in the world, often advising on how to make a deadly weapon out of ordinary objects. In this way, radicalisation reached a further stage, as the idea that much could be done 'from home', wherever in the world their 'home' was located, started to spread. Rumiyah abruptly stopped being released in 2017 for unknown reasons.[34]

Despite using different communicative strategies, all those magazines have a feature in common, i.e., they resemble Western magazines very much in terms of design and visual impact. This choice is not by chance, since, in this way, jihadists make it clear that their goal is to involve in their activities not just those who are geographically, religiously, or culturally close to extremist Islam, but even those living on the side of the world where their 'enemies' are. This feature patently marks the change of vision of terrorists, who have, in the last decades, increasingly tried to attract as adepts even those who were born as part of the 'enemies' (i.e., the Western world).

In addition to magazines, the terrorist 'press' includes other types of publications as well. For instance, several e-books and booklets have been released, both before and after the rise of the Islamic State. Some of them are more focused on the history of jihadist terrorism, glorifying attacks of the past, while others are more religion-based, explaining the basis of Islamic extremism.

Judith Tinnes, *Foreign (Terrorist) Fighters with IS: A European Perspective, International Centre for Counter-Terrorism* (ICCT Press 2015).

[33] Mirom Lakomy, *op. cit.*, 44.

[34] Martina Di Berardino (ed), *ISIS terrore senza confini* (Franco Angeli 2019). See also, generally on the Islamic State's narrative in its magazines, Tim Jacoby, 'The Islamic State's use of the Qur'an in its Magazines, Dabiq and Rumiyah' (2024) 35 Discourse & Society 291.

In general, these magazines and books are not directly accessible through ordinary search engine research – although some issues of Dabiq can even be easily downloaded through Google. Still, as explained above, they are often uploaded on cloud-sharing apps whose links are circulated through instant messaging technologies. Consequently, they can be considered surface web tools, although they can enjoy some level of protection in order not to be easily accessed.

3. THE 'MALICIOUS' USE OF ARTIFICIAL INTELLIGENCE

Until now, this analysis has focused on the use of technology in general, without differentiating between 'ordinary', on the one hand, and 'intelligent' or 'autonomous' tools, on the other hand. Nevertheless, it is a matter of fact that artificial intelligence, i.e., autonomous tools, is increasingly becoming very common in plenty of human activities. Hence, terrorists too are exploiting so-called intelligent algorithms.[35] By referring to 'intelligent algorithms', 'artificial intelligence', or 'artificial intelligence algorithms', we mean all these systems that can perform human-like activities, from simple recognition of texts or audios to full-fledged decision-making in its several forms.

In the wide field of artificial intelligence, there are several sub-fields (see Figure 1.3). The most important ones are machine learning and deep learning. Machine learning is a sub-category of artificial intelligence comprising algorithms that are able to learn from the data they are 'fed' with, without any need for specific instructions given by a human operator. In turn, a sub-group of machine learning algorithms are deep learning algorithms, which are structured in 'networks' resembling human neurones (in fact, these are even called 'neural networks'). Deep learning algorithms mimic the learning process of the human brain, so they are a very advanced form of machine learning.

Given this brief technical introduction, there are several terrorist tactics that can be enhanced by artificial intelligence.

[35] United Nations Office for Counter-Terrorism, UN Counter-Terrorism Centre (CTC), 'Algorithms and Terrorism: The Malicious Use of Artificial Intelligence for Terrorist Purposes' (2021) https://www.un.org/counterterrorism/sites/www.un.org.counterterrorism/files/malicious-use-of-ai-uncct-unicri-report-hd.pdf accessed 31 July 2024.

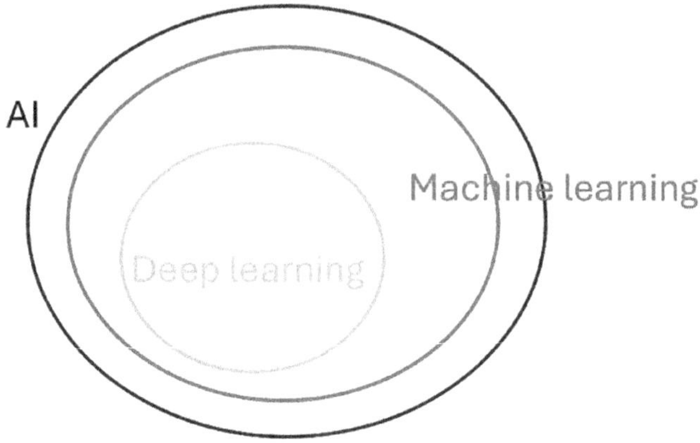

Figure 1.3 *Artificial intelligence*

Again, in the effort to classify, a first distinction can be drawn between those techniques that use artificial intelligence to carry out physical attacks (physical threats of artificial intelligence) and those where algorithms are employed to deploy cyber-attacks (cyber threats of artificial intelligence). Additionally, algorithms can be used to fuel conduct that does not consist of direct attacks (neither in the physical nor in the cyber world), but rather to spread radicalisation or support terrorism. We call these acts 'collateral terrorist activities'. Let us examine these three different groups of methods for using artificial intelligence for terrorist purposes.

3.1 Physical vs. Cyber Attacks

Starting from physical terrorist attacks, algorithms can enable such occurrences in at least three main ways.

First, terrorists can resort to autonomous vehicles.[36] Several types of traditional vehicles – such as cars, vans, trucks – have traditionally been

[36] On autonomous vehicles in general and the legal issues that they raise, Arianna Vedaschi and Gabriele Marino Noberasco, 'Gli autoveicoli a guida autonoma alla prova del diritto' (2019) Diritto pubblico comparato ed europeo (special issue) 769.

used in terrorist attacks.[37] As is well known, the application of artificial intelligence to vehicles led to so-called self-driving cars, in which significant investments have been made by several companies. As is easy to understand, terrorist groups could straightforwardly use these breakthroughs to their advantage, with the vehicle performing the attack without any (at least direct) involvement of a human attacker. The same can be said with regard to other types of vehicles, e.g., planes or ships. Interestingly, this strategy could – at least partially – change and to some extent frustrate the traditional idea of the 'terrorist', normally conceived as a 'suicidal martyr', who is supposed to die in the attack as a result of his extreme sacrifice in the name of jihad.

A second mode to use artificial intelligence to foster physical terrorist attacks is through the use of drones. As scholars studying counterterrorism measures, we are normally used to thinking of drones as powerful – and sometimes legally controversial – tools to fight *against* terrorism. Practices like targeted killings are paradigmatic examples.[38] Nonetheless, it should be considered that drones are at terrorists' disposal too. In this regard, it has been pointed out by a United States-based non-profit organization, the Future of Life Institute,[39] that some terrorist groups are developing 'micro-drones' embedding facial recognition algorithms and carrying a small quantity of explosive. Thanks to facial recognition, these drones would be able to recognise human targets and deploy the explosive against them. Although there is no practical evidence of the actual use of these tools by terrorists, their potential deployment is a cause of concern.[40] Again, and similarly to what has been said regarding autonomous vehicles, this strategy would significantly depart from suicidal attacks usually deployed by terrorists.

A third way in which terrorists are able to resort to artificial intelligence to carry out physical attacks is through the combination of

---

[37] See, e.g., the attack that took place in Nice, France, on 14 July 2016.

[38] Arianna Vedaschi, 'Osama bin Laden: l'ultimo targeted killing. Gli Stati Uniti hanno dunque la licenza di uccidere?' (2011) Diritto pubblico comparato ed europeo 1479; Mary Ellen O'Connell, 'Game of Drones' (2015) 109 AJIL 889.

[39] Slaughterbot, 'Stop Autonomous Weapons', *YouTube* https://www.youtube.com/watch?v=9CO6M2HsoIA accessed 31 July 2024.

[40] Paolo Crippa, 'Cybersecurity and Drones', in Anthony J. Masys (ed), *Handbook of Security Sciences* (Springer 2022) 619.

biotechnology and algorithms, in particular using so-called genetically targeted bio-weapons. In general, the application of algorithms to biotechnology represents a significant advancement in science, leading to positive outcomes in terms of developing therapies, fostering knowledge in the field of genetic research, and so on. However, if put in the hands of terrorists, these biotechnologies might be turned into very dangerous tools. As highlighted by the United Nations Secretary-General in his remarks at the opening of the 2020 Virtual Counter-Terrorism Week,[41] should terrorists gain access to databases of genetic data, they would be able to train algorithms to produce new pathogens and pave the way for bio-terrorist attacks, which could lead to new epidemics or even pandemics.

After analysing the main ways in which artificial intelligence could be used to enhance physical terrorist attacks, the cyber dimension of terrorism vehiculated by artificial intelligence needs to be addressed. Intelligent algorithms could be useful to cyber terrorist attacks in several different ways.

The first method is through denial-of-service incidents.[42] These are attacks aimed at making a computer system connected to the web unavailable by disrupting online services on which it relies. Algorithms can be used in this regard to automate the disruption. In fact, artificial intelligence can be trained to perform the attack instead of the human attacker, making the whole process quick and anonymous. Training an algorithm to achieve this criminal goal is relatively easy and low-cost, so

41 António Guterres, Secretary-General's remarks at the opening of the Virtual Counter-Terrorism Week United Nations [as delivered], 6 July 2020 https://www.un.org/sg/en/content/sg/statement/2020-07-06/secretary-generals-remarks-the-opening-of-the-virtual-counter-terrorism-week-united-nations-delivered accessed 31 July 2024. See also World Health Organisation (WHO), *Biological Weapons* https://www.who.int/health-topics/biological-weapons#tab=tab_1 accessed 5 February 2025. On the risks of bioterrorism before the advent of artificial intelligence, David A. Koplow, 'That Wonderful Year: Smallpox, Genetic Engineering, and Bio-Terrorism' (2003) 62 Md L Rev 417.

42 This type of attack is used even in other ways to destabilise democracy, for instance, during elections. See Philipp M. Lutscher, Nils B. Weidmann, Margaret E. Roberts, Mattijs Jonker, Alistair King, and Alberto Dainotti, 'At Home and Abroad: The Use of Denial-of-service Attacks during Elections in Nondemocratic Regimes' (2020) 64 Journal of Conflict Resolution 373.

this mechanism constitutes a considerable threat. It has been reported[43] that, between 2016 and 2017, the Islamic State launched a series of these 'automated' denial-of-service attacks, targeting several military, economic, and education infrastructures around the world. Similar episodes took place in the following years.[44]

Another very widespread way to leverage intelligent algorithms to organise cyber-terrorist attacks is by resorting to malware. Malware is a category of software that has the ability to bring down or seriously damage a computer system, creating a breach within it and allowing criminal actors to access its data. Unlike denial-of-service, which implies the immediate shutdown of the service, when malware is placed in a system, the user will not notice anything wrong in the functioning of the device and will be able, at least for a certain time, to keep using the system. A specific – and particularly threatening – category of malware is ransomware.[45] A ransomware is a software that encrypts the target's files and asks for a payment (ransom) in order to have the files decrypted. The different types of malware are widely used by 'ordinary' criminals to obtain credit card information, access passwords and other confidential data, read and use the content of emails, and so on. In turn, terrorists can use these tools to access the informatic systems of critical infrastructures, gain sensitive information, even with a view to manipulating it for their purposes. Moreover, when ransomware is used, revenues (the payment of the ransom) can be among the sources to finance terrorist groups and their criminal activities.

Similarly to what has been described above regarding denial of service, artificial intelligence comes into play as machine learning algorithms can be trained on how to build malware and introduce it into a computer system, so the whole process is automatised and de-humanised.[46]

---

[43] Flashpoint Intel Team, 'Cyber Jihadists Dabble in DDoS: Assessing the Threat', *Flashpoint*, 13 July 2017 https://www.flashpoint-intel.com/blog/cyber-jihadists-ddos/ accessed 31 July 2024.

[44] Sam Bocetta and Richard Seroter, 'Has an AI Cyber Attack Happened Yet?', *InfoQ*, 10 March 2020 https://www.infoq.com/articles/ai-cyber-attacks/accessed 31 July 2024.

[45] Asaf Lubin, 'The Law and Politics of Ransomware' (2022) 55 Vand J Transnatl L 1177.

[46] Fabian Teichmann, 'Ransomware Attacks in the Context of Generative Artificial Intelligence – An Experimental Study' (2023) 4 Intl Cybersecurity

Moreover, artificial intelligence can learn how to amplify the effects of malware, for instance by replicating it in other systems and adapting its features to the peculiarities of different informatic environments. Therefore, by integrating artificial intelligence in malware, the consequences can be endemic and tough to manage, especially when the aim of the malware is terrorism and not just ordinary. Moreover, retracing the 'chain of liability' for the setup and deployment of these mechanisms might be particularly hard.

A further possible use of artificial intelligence in the cyber world that can be exploited by terrorists is hacking websites and accounts, including those of social media. Hacking, which can be realised in several automatised ways, e.g., through password guessing algorithms, is a full-fledged form of cyber-attack, although its scope can be more restricted than other cyber-attacks, like, for instance denial-of-service in critical infrastructures. Hacking is extremely useful to terrorists, who, by taking possession of the personal credentials of individuals, can use their webpages and social media accounts to disseminate their message. Artificial intelligence can be helpful when it comes to password guessing: specific types of algorithms, based on the mechanism of neural networks, can be trained through large datasets of passwords, and the algorithm is able to generate from them other versions of those passwords that the human brain could imagine.[47]

Password guessing is indeed not the only technique available to terrorist hackers, as algorithms can be used to break digital mechanisms aimed at protecting systems other than passwords. In this regard, so-called CAPTCHA breaking is illustrative. As known to any internet user, CAPTCHA (an acronym for Completely Automated Public Turing test to tell Computers and Humans Apart) are tools used by websites and other digital platforms to distinguish between human users and robots, thus allowing access to the former while blocking the latter, insofar as these robots are often programmed to spread spam or other unwanted content. CAPTCHA works by asking the user who is trying to access the website to authenticate by solving a challenge, normally consisting of doing something that – at least theoretically – can only be done by a human operator, like recognising a certain object (e.g., a tree) within a series of mixed images. CAPTCHA-breaking algorithms are able to bypass this

L Rev 399.

[47] United Nations Office for Counter-Terrorism, *op. cit.*

scheme since they mimic the human brain and thus are able to correctly solve the challenge launched by the CAPTCHA system. Once deceitfully accessing the system, the algorithm paves the way for carrying out cyber-attacks, disruptions of the platform, or other criminal actions.

Terrorist hackers can also benefit from encryption algorithms. These tools are able to make the content of any digital repository (e.g., email folders, collections of data, etc.) inaccessible from the outside.

3.2 'Collateral' Terrorist Activities

Until this moment, we have addressed the ways in which artificial intelligence can support terrorists in their physical or cybernetic criminal acts. In light of our analysis, there is no doubt that algorithms are really powerful tools in the hand of terrorists when they want to attack civil society through different techniques. Yet, at the same time, it is undeniable that algorithms can be resorted to for other 'collateral' terrorist activities, not consisting of full-fledged attacks but still extremely dangerous for national security. These activities, which can be enhanced by algorithms, are divided into at least three main groups.

The first group of 'collateral' terrorist activities that can be empowered by artificial intelligence is the spread of terrorist propaganda,[48] embedded in that idea of 'radicalisation' to which we referred earlier in this analysis. Differently from some of the other uses of artificial intelligence that have been described until now, which are more potential than actual, terrorists are already strongly relying on intelligent algorithms to spread their propaganda. One of the most effective tools in this regard, from the perspective of terrorists, is so-called deep fakes.[49] Deep fakes are

---

[48] Chinasa Susan Adigwe, Nanyeneke Ravana Mayeke, Samuel Oladiipo Olabanji, Olalekan J. Okunleye, Princess Joeaneke, and Oluwaseun Oladeji Olaniyi, 'The Evolution of Terrorism in the Digital Age: Investigating the Adaptation of Terrorist Groups to Cyber Technologies for Recruitment, Propaganda, and Cyberattacks', 20 February 2024 https://papers.ssrn.com/sol3/papers.cfm?abstract_id=4756964 accessed 31 July 2024.

[49] This has been particularly common in far-right terrorism and extremism. See Ella Busch and Jacob Ware, 'The Weaponisation of Deepfakes', International Center for Counter-Terrorism Policy Brief (December 2023) https://www.icct.nl/sites/default/files/2023-12/The%20Weaponisation%20of%20Deepfakes.pdf accessed 31 July 2024.

contents of different types (audios, videos, photos, etc.) completely created by artificial intelligence. In this context, the intelligent algorithm, having real contents as a starting basis (e.g., an existing photo, a video, etc.), is able to generate new content, which is fake even if highly realistic or at least very plausible. Deep fakes could be used, among others, to generate fake videos of political leaders who incite hatred toward a certain community, thus increasing outrage against 'ordinary politics', something that fuels people's interest in 'alternative' institutional settings (as terrorism often presents itself) and, ultimately, might urge them to radicalisation. In other words, deep fakes are an 'advanced' form of fake news. Deep fakes, as well as intelligent chatbots such as ChatGPT,[50] can also be used to create customised radicalisation narratives and messages, through which terrorists can build 'micro-targeted' strategies, namely strategies that are tailor-made for single categories of users or even individual users.

The second group of collateral terrorist activities to be enhanced by artificial intelligence is the collection of financial resources to fund terrorist organisations. Terrorists can leverage intelligent algorithms to get money to finance their activities, and the most important method to do so is crypto-trade. As widely known, cryptocurrencies (i.e., virtual currencies that exist virtually, are convertible, and use cryptography to secure transactions) are nowadays used globally, and this is not necessarily for criminal or other illegal purposes. In the context of crypto-trade activities (including those that are perfectly lawful), artificial intelligence may play a pivotal role, for example by being trained by financial actors to make market speculations and forecasts, thereby optimising the trade of cryptocurrencies. Within this scenario, there are some hints that terrorist groups – or even individuals – are starting to use cryptocurrencies and their associated algorithms to fund themselves. Suffice it to say that in 2020 more than 1 million USD in cryptocurrencies was seized by US authorities from accounts associated with the Islamic State, Al-Qaeda,

[50] Gabriel Weimann, Alexander Pack, Rapaport Gal, Joelle Scheinin, David Diaz, and Rachel Sulciner, 'Generating Terror: The Risks of Generative AI Exploitation', Reichman University International Institute for Counter-Terrorism (ICT), 28 January 2024 https://ict.org.il/generating-terror-the-risks-of-generative-ai-exploitation/ accessed 31 July 2024.

and other minor terrorist organisations.[51] Other sources[52] allege that even earlier, at the time of the 2015 Paris attacks, part of the financial resources that made the well-known awful events possible was raised through bitcoins. These claims have admittedly not been demonstrated yet. In sum, although there is no large amount of evidence that terrorists are widely resorting to crypto-trading, its potential is undoubtedly a serious concern.

The third and last group of terrorist activities to be efficiently 'boosted' by artificial intelligence is disguising terrorists' identities. As easy to imagine, terrorists often need to show false identities when travelling from one place to another to plan and perform attacks, spread radicalisation, and, more generally, carry out their criminal activities. Nonetheless, many of them are already filed in databases held by law enforcement bodies and intelligence authorities from all over the world and would be immediately matched if they openly used their true identities and travelling documents. To circumvent this risk, they might employ algorithms to create fake passports. This is possible through a technology called MorGAN (MORphing through Generative Adversarial Networks), which can give rise to 'morphed passports'.[53] More in detail, MorGAN can merge biometric data gathered from the images displayed on the passports of two or more persons, creating a new, counterfeited one, that

---

[51] Andy Greenberg, 'ISIS Allegedly Ran a Covid-19 PPE Scam Site', *Wired*, 13 August 2020 https://www.wired.com/story/isis-allegedly-ran-a-covid-19-ppe-scam-site/?utm_medium=social&utm_source=twitter&utm_brand=wired&utm_social-type=owned&mbid=social_twitter accessed 31 July 2024.

[52] Chainalysis Team, 'Fact Checking Recent Cryptocurrency Terrorism Financing Reports', Chainalysis, 20 May 2020 https:// blog.chainalysis.com/reports/cryptocurrency-terrorism-financing-fact-check accessed 31 July 2024.

[53] On morphed passports, literature is particularly wide from the viewpoint of computer scientists. Among others: Erion-Vasilis Pikoulis, Zafeiria-Marina Ioannou, Mersini Paschou, and Evangelos Sakkopoulos, 'Face Morphing, a Modern Threat to Border Security: Recent Advances and Open Challenges' (2021) 11 Applied Sciences (p. 3207); Franziska Schwarz, Klaus Schwarz, and Reiner Creutzburg, 'Improving Detection of Manipulated Passport Photos – Training Course for Border Control Inspectors to Detect Morphed Facial Passport Photos' (2021) Society for Imaging Science and Technology 136.

can be suitable for the two (or even more) individuals, and is normally able to pass security checks (e.g., at airports). In other cases, an algorithm can make an existing passport (for instance, stolen from a person who is not suspected of terrorism) suitable for two people (its legitimate owner *and* the terrorist or suspected terrorist). In both cases, creating a morphed passport is a very sophisticated and complex process. In order to successfully generate a working fake passport, it is not sufficient to print fake photographs and combine them with false personal data. This is because, when a passport is scanned at border control, an algorithm matches the biometric features of the traveller (by taking a photo or video of him/her) with those of the photo displayed on the passport. Therefore, the morphed photo has to be similar enough to the facial features of the traveller to cheat the algorithm used at border controls; and at the same time, it has to be different enough from the true document of the traveller (who is a terrorist) to avoid matching with the photo contained in the databases available to border control authorities, which would recognise that person as a criminal or suspected criminal, block him from travelling, and interrogate or even arrest him.

It is worth noting that morphed passports, although created through algorithms that might be available on the surface layers of the web, are almost always traded and exchanged on the so-called dark web.[54] The same can be said regarding the terrorist trade of cryptocurrencies, addressed above, since their market is a relevant part of the dark web. This means that there are some technology terrorist tools that work on the boundaries between the surface and dark web, both functional to their deployment. This feature leads us directly to examine the next topic of this analysis, which is the use of the dark web by terrorists.

4. THE USE OF THE DARK WEB BY TERRORISTS

The activities carried out by terrorists on the dark web are usually those that would immediately entail criminal investigation and, possibly, prosecution if performed on the surface web or in any other 'open' digital or physical environment, so they absolutely need to be hidden. In other

[54] For a wide explanation of how terrorist financing runs through the dark web, see Doron Goldbarsht, 'Dancing in the Dark: Terrorist Financing Via the Dark Web', in Doron Goldbarsht and Loui de Koker (eds), *Financial Crime and the Law* (Springer 2024) 167.

terms, terrorists use the dark web to carry out those activities, embedded in their plans and programs, that are most patently illegal. This is consistent with the fact, mentioned above, that the dark web consists of those web layers that cannot be accessed by ordinary search engines – so special software is needed, such as TOR (an acronym for The Onion Router). Thus, the dark web considerably favours the secrecy that is needed in cases of undoubtedly illegal behaviour and makes the interception of activities carried out thereon unlikely, although not totally impossible.[55]

Due to the very fact that the dark web is surrounded by secrecy and inscrutability, and that some of its layers are unknown as to their content or even to their existence, it is extremely complex to list with absolute precision *all* the activities that terrorists perform on the deepest and most concealed levels of the net. Nonetheless, some of them are ascertained, thanks to units of law enforcement and intelligence services who make all possible efforts to access and scan the dark web to monitor, investigate, and prosecute these conducts.[56]

Firstly, the dark web is demonstrably used by terrorists for the exchange of illegal materials. As mentioned above, these materials can be wholly virtual (such as cryptocurrencies, useful to finance terrorism) or physical objects (for example, morphed passports, weapons, and other items that can be used to build them, along with their instructions). These full-fledged 'dark markets' often include other illicit content that are not directly related to terrorism (such as drugs, child pornography materials, etc.), and the only way to discover them is through operational analysis carried out by specialised cyber-crime units of police and intelligence forces. In 2021, Europol coordinated a joint international operation – involving authorities from Australia, Denmark, Germany, Moldova, Ukraine, the United Kingdom, and the United States – which managed to take down one of the world's largest illegal markets on the dark web,

---

[55] See Babak Akhgar, Marco Gercke, Stefanos Vrochidis, and Helen Gibson (eds), *Dark Web Investigation* (Springer 2021); Jaspal Kaur Saini and Divya Bansal, 'Detecting Online Recruitment of Terrorists: Towards Smarter Solutions to Counter Terrorism' (2021) 13 Intl J Inf Techn 697.

[56] Gabriel Weimann, 'Going Darker? The Challenge of Dark Net Terrorism' (2018) Woodrow Wilson Centre Press https://cris.haifa.ac.il/en/publications/going-darker-the-challenge-of-dark-net-terrorism accessed 31 July 2024.

where transactions also included the exchange of physical and digital terrorist material. Nevertheless, markets like this continuously proliferate in the deepest portions of the net and sometimes remain concealed for a long time, so keeping up with all of them is hardly ever possible even for organised and well-functioning investigating authorities.

Secondly, the dark web allows terrorists to communicate in a 'safer' (from their own viewpoint) way, compared to communication on the surface web. Safer communication means that they can upload more explicit content and, in general, carry out more 'aggressive' forms of radicalisation strategies. For instance, they often set up full-fledged 'training courses' for prospective recruits, available on dark web platforms, where they explain how to become part of extremist groups both practically (e.g., by pointing out how to assemble and use explosives, build bombs, carry out attacks, etc.) and ideologically (e.g., through sermons, preaching, and other speeches containing incitement, violent videos, etc.). In this way, terrorists manage to recruit their adepts more directly than they can on the surface web. According to sociological studies,[57] this type of recruitment is also statistically more effective in attracting people, partly because those who surf the dark web in search of this type of content are normally already 'on the route' towards radicalisation, so are more easily swayed by this type of narrative. Furthermore, terrorist communication taking place on the dark web can also be aimed at objectives other than 'mere' radicalisation and recruitment. As a matter of fact, the dark web is often the virtual venue where terrorists gather in order to concretely organise physical and non-physical attacks (cyber-planning).

Thirdly, the dark web is sometimes used also as a channel to broadcast even real scenes of live attacks. This happened, for example, during an attack carried out in Pakistan in 2017, when the perpetrators attached smartphones to their bodies and broadcasted the whole action on the dark web.[58] Although live broadcasting of attacks can be considered as a form of communication (thus, it could be included in what we listed as the second 'stream' of terrorist activities on the dark web), it undoubtedly carries a distinct (and stronger) impact on viewers, so we decided

---

[57] Hsinchun Chen, 'Sentiment and Affect Analysis of Dark Web Forums: Measuring Radicalisation on the Internet' (2008) IEEE International Conference on Intelligence and Security Informatics, Taipei, Taiwan, 2008.

[58] Rafat Mahmood and Michael Jetter, 'Communications Technology and Terrorism' (2020) 64 Journal of Conflict Resolution 127.

to consider it as a separate category. Similarly, the 2019 shooting in Christchurch (New Zealand)[59] was livestreamed on Facebook and, after being removed by the platform, the video shifted to the dark web.

The most serious concern raised by the dark web is that, despite the existence of specialised law enforcement and intelligence units and ad hoc methods to scan it, there is no limit to the 'layers' that can be added to the web, since a new, disguised 'level' can always be created, giving rise to an endless chain. Consequently, this characteristic of the dark web constitutes one of the hardest challenges in the struggle against terrorist activities carried out on the dark web, although some measures have been framed, as will be clarified in Part II.

However, as hard as it is to chase terrorists on the dark web, it must be said that, at least, this is still part of the *real* digital world. Things have changed – and have become even more complicated – when terrorists move – and it is very likely that they do so – their criminal conduct to the so-called metaverse. This is the topic we analyse in the subsequent chapter.

[59] David Lowe, 'Christchurch Terrorist Attack, The Far-Right and Social Media: What Can We Learn?' (2019) The New Jurist 1; Minttu Tikka, Johanna Sumiala, Anu A. Harju, and Katja Valaskivi, 'Weaponization of Liveness: Streaming Death as a Hybrid Media Event of Terrorist Violence' (2020) AoIR Selected Papers of Internet Research 1.

2. The use of technology in terrorist activities in the metaverse

As hinted by the definition of the metaverse reported above, this concept refers to an augmented reality that allows the user not just to interact with something (images, scripts, other users, etc.), but to be put in the middle of an action and become part of it, as if they were in a different world, living in parallel with the real one. To be more precise, some features characterising the metaverse have been identified:[1] it is persistent and immersive, meaning that it feels real and has the scale and form of a separate world or universe; it is synchronous, i.e., it allows real-time experiences; it merges the digital world with the physical one, giving rise to situations that may have effects on both; it gives birth to its own economy, where individuals can conduct business, produce and sell values, create unlimited new wealth, and set up new markets; it is interoperable, meaning its data, contents, and assets can be available across several platforms, making interactions smoother. The metaverse is still widely unregulated from a legal angle:[2] except for general principles of single fields where it is developed, there is no specific norm applying to this 'new universe'.

Even from a practical view, implementation of the metaverse is definitely not completed yet. Some social media platforms – e.g., Facebook, part of the Meta group – are examining the possibility of introducing

[1] Analysis and Research Team (ART) of the EU General Secretariat of the Council, 'Metaverse–Virtual world, Real challenges', ART Paper 9 March 2022 https://data.consilium.europa.eu/doc/document/ST-9292-2022-INIT/en/pdf accessed 31 July 2024.

[2] Literature on the legal regulation of the metaverse is still scarce and some works are forthcoming. Nizan Geslevich Packin, *The Cambridge Handbook of Law and Policy for NFTs* (CUP 2024); Larry A. Di Matteo and Michel Cannarsa (eds), *Research Handbook of Metaverse and Law* (Edward Elgar 2024).

metaverse interfaces, and, at the time of writing this book, this process has not been completed yet by any of the so-called big techs.

In the future, the metaverse is foreseen to be used for a wide range of different purposes, some of which have not even been identified yet, as this tool is still under continuous development.[3] The current state of the art shows that it could be employed for a variety of activities: among others, gaming (which is the field in which it is currently more advanced); development of work tools; e-commerce; design; e-fitness and other forms of entertainment; and several others. Nevertheless, in addition to these perfectly lawful uses (and many others that are being and will be developed), the metaverse can also be exploited for criminal aims. All the possible ways to use the metaverse by terrorists have not been tangibly put into practice yet, but 'there is potential for the metaverse to become a new domain for terrorist activity', as warned by the National Counterterrorism Innovation, Technology and Education Centre[4] (Nebraska, United States). Specifically, the metaverse, with its peculiar features, is likely to expose new (or new forms of) vulnerabilities of users, which were not so evident in the real digital world, on which terrorists could leverage.

Based on available studies on the relationship between the metaverse and national security threats, especially terrorism, we have identified three broad areas where the metaverse could empower the actions of terrorists. These are: radicalisation efforts (including through so-called desensitisation); training activities and/or attack planning; terrorist financing. These areas are the 'metaverse-based equivalent' of some of the terrorist tactics addressed before and performed by terrorists in the 'ordinary' digital world. This correspondence demonstrates how some activities – including terrorist ones – carried out in the real digital world can be easily 'moved' to the new scenario constituted by the metaverse; in turn, this means that an 'augmented reality', as the metaverse is, is able to enhance people's perception and way of acting, as already

---

[3] Gabriel Weimann and Roy Dimant, 'The Metaverse and Terrorism: Threats and Challenges' (2023) 17 Perspectives on Terrorism 92.

[4] Joel S. Elson, Austin C. Doctor and Sam Hunter, 'The Metaverse Offers a Future Full of Potential – for Terrorists and Extremists, too', *The Conversation*, 7 January 2022 https://theconversation.com/the-metaverse-offers-a-future-full-of-potential-for-terrorists-and-extremists-too-173622 accessed 31 July 2024.

demonstrated by psychology and behavioural studies that are starting to gain interest in this field.[5] The following sections analyse each of the three mentioned areas of potential interplay between the metaverse and national security threats.

1. INDOCTRINATING AND RADICALISING IN THE METAVERSE: 'NEW PATHS'?

Through the metaverse, it is likely that terrorist groups will be able to convene live virtual communities, living and acting in parallel with real ones. In other words, terrorists may try to obtain, by way of the metaverse, what, until now, they have failed to achieve in the real world, i.e., achieving their state-like and society-like ambitions. Building a virtual society in the metaverse, organising virtual meetings in which people can participate not just remotely with their video and audio (as if they were in a Zoom call) but as active parts of them, and, in general turning their 'ideological' narrative into concrete scenarios makes the 'terrorist alternative' more attractive to people, as the metaverse would enhance terrorists' ability to manipulate emotions. Consequently, terrorist radicalisation strategies might become more successful and have a sort of multiplier effect, thus becoming endemic. Notably, it would become extremely challenging to distinguish the 'ordinary' reality from the 'augmented' reality, so actions performed in the metaverse could have serious consequences on the real world as well, without people fully realising it.

Moreover, scholars[6] noticed that, through the metaverse combined with artificial intelligence, it would be possible to simulate – thanks to elements like avatars – a realistic resurrection of late leaders of terrorism, such as Osama Bin Laden, Abu Bakr al-Baghdadi, and others, allowing their adepts to interact with them as if they were alive. Undoubtedly, this aspect would strengthen the sense of 'community' among terrorists, galvanise their supporters, and thus increase the popularity and positive outcome of radicalisation strategies.

Furthermore, the metaverse could also boost the spread of radicalisation conveyed through disinformation, fake news, and tools like

---

[5] Jeanne F. Brockmeyer, 'Desensitization and Violent Video Games: Mechanisms and Evidence' (2022) 31 Child and Adolescent Psychiatric Clinics of North America 121.

[6] Gabriel Weimann, Roy Dimant, *op. cit.*

deepfakes (already discussed above in the part dedicated to the 'real digital world'). In fact, through the metaverse, it would be possible to simulate fake or manipulated scenarios, which more vulnerable individuals could mistakenly exchange for real situations. Ultimately, the metaverse might make the spread of disinformation, fake news, and deepfakes more realistic and easier to believe.

Another way to foster radicalisation is through so-called desensitisation, and the metaverse may play a pivotal role in this regard as well. Although partially different from those explained until this moment, desensitisation is a considerable risk. It is a phenomenon that existed well before we started to even imagine the metaverse, and it could be strongly enhanced by the metaverse itself. As a sociological and psychological phenomenon, desensitisation has been described since the 1990s with regard to exposure to violent situations, be they real or simulated. In particular, desensitisation refers to the fact that, if a person is put in continuous connection with violent scenarios, his or her sensitivity and perception of violence and empathy with the victims will decrease because the person will become accustomed to violence. In other terms, desensitisation leads to some sort of normalisation of violence to which someone is constantly exposed. For example, this desensitisation effect has been demonstrated by several studies conducted on young people using violent videogames.[7] These people tended to care less about other persons' feelings and emotions and were more likely to engage in dangerous and violent activities themselves, no longer in a video game, but in the real world. This process, as described (from violent video games, to desensitisation, to actual violence) was demonstrated by scientists to have been caused by full-fledged effects of visualised violence on their brains. To some extent, this phenomenon of desensitisation could be traced back to the so-called broken windows theory, according to which getting accustomed to a demoted environment may increase criminality and, in general, violence.

It has been reported[8] that the metaverse could increase the effects of desensitisation, as an 'augmented reality', detached from the real world

---

7 Jeanne Funk F. Brockmyer, 'Desensitization and Violent Video Games: Mechanisms and Evidence' (2022) 31 Child and Adolescent Psychiatric Clinics of North America 131.

8 Kieron Allen, 'How Desensitization Through Immersion Could Have Real-World Consequences', *Acceleration Economy*, 22 April 2022 https://

and its functioning, could disengage people from their moral and ethical constraints. Loosening these limits may make a person more prone to embrace extremist and violent behaviour and ideas, so, in short, to become radicalised if exposed to terrorist content and ideologies. This is due to the immersive features of the metaverse (made possible, e.g., through the use of avatars), which make people feel as if they were part of the situations they are experiencing, including the most violent ones. Desensitisation in the metaverse could thus facilitate mobilisation of radicalised adepts to carry out attacks, determine their determination to spread propaganda, approach other radicalised people, and engage in other terrorist behavior. In other words, there is a cause-effect link between desensitisation and radicalisation and, in turn, between the advent of the metaverse and desensitisation.

2. TRAINING ACTIVITIES AND ATTACK PLANNING: WHAT CHANGES WITH THE METAVERSE?

Besides working as an amplifier for radicalisation strategies, the metaverse could be an additional tool to support and enhance full-fledged practical activities, such as the training of those who have been radicalised and even the planning of attacks.

As regards the training, by creating a sort of 'parallel universe', the metaverse could offer an environment to simulate physical and cyber-attacks, deployment and construction of weapons, and all those activities that are needed to put the terrorist ideology 'into practice'. Due to augmented emotional and physical involvement that it provides, as remarked several times, the metaverse can be defined as an 'immersive' environment; as a result, training adepts there could be much more effective and efficient than doing so in the traditional digital setting, which is definitely not able to guarantee the same level of engagement. Additionally, these simulations – at least as long as they remain such – could be carried out in secret and without causing any fuss, so terrorists would be allowed to engage in their training undisturbed.

As far as the planning and coordination of attacks are concerned, the metaverse could be useful to terrorists, first of all, to circumvent ordinary

---

accelerationeconomy.com/metaverse/how-desensitization-through-immersion-could-have-real-world-consequences/ accessed 31 July 2024.

communication channels and so avert surveillance measures adopted by authorities.[9] Actually, at least so far, surveillance strategies, although very refined, are mainly aimed at targeting the ordinary digital world, and so the metaverse could partially escape them.

Additionally, augmented reality could provide terrorists with the possibility of staging the attack, studying the features of the environment in which they are going to act, and averting potential risks. In other words, they would be in the condition of making a 'rehearsal' of the attack, assessing how to make it work best.

Furthermore, the metaverse could give terrorists the opportunity to identify new targets when planning attacks. In clearer words, terrorists could target not only events and infrastructures that exist in the real world, but also those having their place in the metaverse. These actions could bring serious harm in spite of the fact that the targets only exist in 'another' reality. For instance – as noted by the Council of the European Union in a recent report trying to address the possible terrorist use of the metaverse[10] – if a terrorist group shoots down avatars in the metaverse, this has no practical consequences, yet could have relevant psychological effects on civil society. This is especially true where the attack carried out in the metaverse is widely advertised, something that terrorists normally do. Therefore, although taking place only in the 'parallel world' created by the metaverse, such attacks would have undeniable effects in the real world.

In the next section, we see how, according to a similar pattern, even virtual currencies can have huge consequences on the real world and, most of all, on national security. This happens in particular when cryptocurrencies are used in the metaverse.

---

[9] Council of the European Union, EU Counter-Terrorism Coordinator, *The Metaverse in the Context of the Fight Against Terrorism*, 9292/22, 2 June 2022 https://data.consilium.europa.eu/doc/document/ST-9292-2022-INIT/en/pdf accessed 31 July 2024.

[10] Ibid.

3. TERRORIST FINANCING IN THE METAVERSE: ENHANCING THE MALICIOUS USE OF CRYPTO-CURRENCIES

We have already highlighted, in the sections dedicated to the 'real digital world', the serious risks lying behind the use of cryptocurrencies by terrorists. If cryptocurrencies are already potentially dangerous in the 'traditional' dimension, the metaverse could work as a 'detonator' in this regard, seriously fuelling digital terrorism. In fact, cryptocurrencies are at the very foundation of the metaverse, insofar as owning a cryptocurrency wallet to hold digital assets will most likely be a requirement for everyone willing to access this new dimension. Therefore, the metaverse bolsters the creation of a parallel economic system, in which all the measures – e.g., financial blacklists, anti-money laundering tools, etc. – established until now in the real world to counter terrorism financing are likely to be poorly effective. This new economic environment will – at least at the beginning, i.e., until the metaverse is legally regulated – guarantee anonymity, lack of oversight, and its transactions will not be traceable, something that is highly convenient for terrorist fundraising. Additionally, it may make these transactions increasingly more part of the economy, with adverse implications even on ordinary and real economic activities.

A final overview on technology as a terrorist tool

Some important aspects of the relationship between technology, including intelligent algorithms, and terrorist activities have been pointed out thanks to the analysis carried out in the previous chapters.

The first is that the more technology is developed, the clearer its well-known 'neutral' dimension is highlighted. As we have discussed in the introduction to this book, technology is neither good nor evil per se; rather, it is a neutral tool, and it actually all depends on how it is going to be used, by whom, in what circumstances, and above all, for what purposes. As a matter of fact, when we talk about technology and terrorism, what immediately comes to our minds is the use of technology to *fight against* terrorism. In this regard, technology has an undoubtedly 'bright side', since it aims at fighting one of the most frightening and terrible threats of our times, as we extensively explain in the remainder of this volume (Part II).

Nevertheless, the study we conducted so far has clarified how many malicious terrorist purposes technology may serve, thus shedding light on its 'dark side'. This is actually nothing new, since the double-edged nature of technology has been widely discussed even before the spread of artificial intelligence algorithms. However, the current breakthroughs in technology emphasise this double dimension, making it evident that how technology is *regulated* might really make a difference. Actually, if regulators – cooperating with the 'giants of technology' – manage to control most technological applications, room for terrorists will be reduced or at least better monitored. As we point out in Part II, we are far from reaching this objective in terms of regulation.

The second important aspect that arises from this first part of our volume is that terrorists are normally more rapid in finding ways in which technology may bring benefits to their criminal aims than are public authorities in developing counter-measures based on the same technology. This is mainly due to the fact that, unlike public authorities, terrorists do not have to comply with legal requirements and caveats when they develop technological tools. For instance, while public authorities – as well as private entities working in the field of technology – have to adhere to basic privacy and data protection guarantees, this is not a concern for terrorists. Additionally, while public authorities – and anyone else who develops technological tools for lawful purposes – have to carry out trials and assess the impact of their devices, terrorists are not obligated to do so, and this results in increased speed. Many more examples of this kind could be given.

The third relevant remark is that, notwithstanding the challenges that law faces in keeping pace with the evolution of technology, the described scenario, showing the technology environment mastered more and more by terrorists in professional and efficient ways, calls for a strong reaction by those who fight against terrorism. In other words, the efficiency and effectiveness of technologies available to counter-actors should be at least at the same level as the technology at the disposal of terrorists. Yet, this is made very complicated by the above-mentioned factors, i.e., that, while terrorists are 'free' to develop efficient technologies since they do not need to care about respect for rights and freedom, regulators have much tighter legal constraints.

Last but not least, we think that the analysis we conducted about the terrorist use of technology may lead us to rethink the very concept of emergency. While at the beginning – meaning in the aftermath of 9/11 – we were naturally driven to think that the emergency was constituted by terrorism per se, the scenario is far more complicated nowadays. In fact, the pervasiveness and the potential embedded in technology tools may constitute an emergency as well if such technology falls 'into the wrong hands', that is to say, the hands of terrorists. Hence, technology may end up being an emergency itself, although a more nuanced one and, what is more important, 'convertible' into useful tools to counter the threat. How technology can undergo this 'conversion', what are the risks, what is the state of the art of regulation and jurisprudence about it is exactly the aim of Part II of this book.

Appendix to Part I: a taxonomy of the terrorist use of technology

Table A1.1 A taxonomy of the terrorist use of technology

'Real' digital world	Metaverse
Main features: • The environment is digital, but with effects on real life • The digital environment is not immersive • Activities can take place in the surface web or in deeper layers of the web. A mix of both can happen as well • Resort to artificial intelligence is increasing	Main features: • The environment is digital and characterised by so-called augmented reality • Immersive digital environment, considered as the 'evolution' of the internet • It allows users to enter a 'parallel' world • Synchronous and real-time experience • It merges the 'real' and the 'digital' world • Still under development
Main activities: • Radicalisation and indoctrination • Terrorist press • Dark web • Malicious use of artificial intelligence	Main activities: • New paths of radicalisation and indoctrination • Training and attack planning

Source: Authors (through Microsoft Word).

PART II

Technology as a ‘counter-terrorism tool’

A general introductory overview: technology as a tool to respond to terrorism

As extensively explained in Part I, the use that terrorists have been making of technology is highly pervasive and refined, including the most advanced tools to ruthlessly carry out their destructive strategies.

Given that scenario, to effectively fight terrorism, those bodies tasked with *countering* it – first of all, public authorities – must have at their disposal a technology arsenal at least as performant as the one owned by terrorists. As a matter of fact, if counter-terrorism strategies did not rely on technology, terrorists would hold an unacceptable competitive advantage. For this reason, since the very beginning of the 'war on terror',[1] technology has played a key role in framing legal measures against terrorism.[2]

Since the struggle against international terrorism began more than twenty years ago,[3] it is not difficult to understand that the techniques to

[1] The idea of the struggle against terrorism as 'war' was theorised by the Bush Administration in the aftermath of the 9/11 attacks. See George W. Bush, Address to a Joint Session of Congress and the American People, 20 September 2001. On the approaches to the 'war on terror', Arianna Vedaschi, À la guerre comme à la guerre*? La disciplina della guerra nel diritto costituzionale comparato* (Giappichelli 2007) 504; Federico Fabbrini and Vicki C. Jackson (eds), *Constitutionalism Across Borders in the Struggle Against Terrorism* (Edward Elgar 2016).

[2] Among the first analyses about technology and terrorism at the beginning of the fight against terror: Michael Herman, 'Counter-Terrorism, Information Technology and Intelligence Change' (2003) 18 Intelligence and National Security 40.

[3] Arianna Vedaschi and Kim Lane Scheppele (eds), *9/11 and the Rise of Global Anti-Terrorism Law: How the UN Security Council Rules the World* (CUP 2021).

counter this threat through technology have evolved consequently and relevantly. It could be said that there was a mutual relation, as the need to deal with terrorism fostered the development of technology, and the other way around, creating a sort of synergy.

In this part, we pursue two main purposes. The first is to make an effort to categorise all the possible uses of technology as a counter-terrorism tool according to their prevailing aim. We refer to 'prevailing' aim since – as will become clearer in the following sections – there are some tools that serve more than one aim, or there are strong interrelations between several purposes; nevertheless, we tried to detect which is the one that predominates over the others. The second objective, in parallel with this classification, is to take stock of the 'state of the art' of technological advances and shed light on the main legal issues, with a view to suggesting potential guidelines on how to combine a human rights-driven approach with the essential need to ensure a high level of technological advancement in counter-terrorism measures, which cannot be set aside.

Starting from the categorisation, we can pinpoint three main clusters of counter-terrorism measures embedding technology, differentiating themselves based on their main purpose. A first group of technologies is used to identify the kind of threat: these techniques scan the environment (both the physical and the digital one) to track possible signs of threats to security. The technologies of this first group are even able, in some cases and through different mechanisms, to assess the level of risk embodied in people, communication, or other items they identify. More clearly, these tools are able to evaluate the likelihood that a certain person, situation, or element may turn out to be a danger, by analysing and grading pre-identified 'risk factors'. In general, the more advanced the algorithm is, the higher the assessment capacity of the tool proves to be. These technologies take a preventive stance: they scan, identify, and assess generally *everyone*, not only the people who are already suspected of terrorism or related crimes. Although they embed significant potential in preventing dangerous acts from taking place, they may infringe on basic principles of the rule of law – let us just think of the presumption of innocence—as will be clarified in the remainder of the analysis.

More in detail, when the need to fight terrorism is at stake, the first step is to identify who and what can turn out to be a threat, how this threat could spread, and generally, what its dynamics are. At the identification stage, technology can help in several ways, and all of them can be brought back to the idea of mass surveillance.[4] Mass surveillance can be defined as a type of generalised surveillance, meaning that it does not target a particular person suspected of having committed a crime or having links with a criminal organisation; rather, mass surveillance aims at scanning the activities of all individuals without differentiating between those who are suspected of having committed a crime or are about to commit it and those who are not. The main purpose of mass surveillance is to profile people and detect potentially suspicious behaviour. Undoubtedly, surveillance is the most preventive form of counter-terrorism activity: not only is there no committed act of terrorism (yet), but there is even no specific suspected person (or group of persons, e.g., Muslims). Actually, it is easy to see how this feature may clash with the principle of the presumption of innocence, at the very foundation of any rule-of-law-based legal system.[5]

This activity of generalised surveillance can take different forms. Based on the features of each form, we can single out at least three main types of mass surveillance, which we analyse in chronological order (i.e., from the most traditional one, not necessarily relying on 'intelligent' technology, to the most cutting-edge).

The first and most accustomed type of mass surveillance refers to the collection and retention of communication data. More precisely, it is not the *content* of communication exchanged that is targeted and gathered – otherwise, such a procedure would fall within the category of interception, which we classify as a 'chasing' tool, to be addressed in a dedicated section. Rather, what is gathered in this context belongs to the category of 'metadata', meaning the data *about* the communication, detached from its content, as will be better explained *infra*. This type of mass surveillance, consisting of metadata collection, can be classified as a quite 'traditional' one, insofar as it does not necessarily need

[4] On the socio-economic aspects of mass surveillance, see Shoshana Zuboff, *The Age of Surveillance Capitalism: The Fight for a Human Future at the New Frontier of Power* (Public Affairs 2019). For a general legal analysis of several mass surveillance techniques, see David Gray (ed), *The Cambridge Handbook of Surveillance* Law (CUP 2017).

[5] Arianna Vedaschi and Valerio Lubello, 'Data Retention and its Implications for the Fundamental Right to Privacy. A European Perspective' (2015) 10 Tilburg LR 14, 25.

algorithms to work (although 'algorithmic' forms of metadata surveillance[6] have recently been elaborated, and we will focus on them *infra*).

The second category of identifying technology tools can be classified as 'intermediate' in terms of technology advancement. It includes those technologies that are able to scan the web in order to find out whether any dangerous content is aimed at radicalising internet users. This scanning strategy can be further sub-divided into two limbs: on the one hand, the suspected dangerous content is flagged, and this is a purely identification measure; on the other hand, if the danger is confirmed as potentially such, the content is removed, and the account of the person who posted it can be suspended, based on the policies or terms of service of the hosting web platform.[7]

The third and most advanced method consists of scanning and collecting a particularly sensitive category of data, that is biometric data; the collection of biometric data is done above all through facial images, but other features ascribable to biometrics can also be resorted to, such as irises, voices, or fingerprints.

We dedicate Chapters 3, 4, and 5 to this first group of technologies.

A second group of technologies is those aimed at chasing the threat. The verb 'to chase' is used here to point out that we are outside of the 'preventive' aim, characterising the first group, and shift to a group of technologies that applies to people who are already identified and assessed as a threat. Thus, these people are already suspected or even convicted. These tools are available especially to law enforcement bodies and are employed to investigate suspects or even to make sure that convicted people no longer constitute a threat. This group includes quite 'traditional' technologies, on which we decided not to focus in order to give more room to the most cutting-edge ones that are being developed or updated even while this book is being written. Chapter 6 is focused on this group of technologies.

---

[6] This type of surveillance has been defined as algorithmic by both computer scientists and legal scholars, and is a terminology widely used in interdisciplinary publications. See, among others, Maria Helen Murphy, 'Algorithmic Surveillance: The Collection Conundrum' (2017) 31 International Review of Law, Computers & Technology 225.

[7] Chiara Graziani, 'Removing Terrorist Content Online. The Intersection between the International, Regional, and Domestic Level', in Arianna Vedaschi, Kim Lane Scheppele, *op. cit.*, 222.

The third group of technologies that we address are those designed to shape public opinion. These technologies, which gained momentum in the post-9/11 era, are useful to public authorities for depicting terrorists as 'enemies' and, in general, for preventing people from falling into the pitfalls of terrorism. Therefore, tools enhancing counter-radicalisation, de-radicalisation, and prevention of radicalisation fall within this cluster. Chapter 7 addresses this group of technologies.

In our research, we examine each of these categories and, in giving examples, we apply a comparative methodology. According to this method, the analysis is focused on the main Western liberal democracies and other countries that are methodologically comparable with them, in coherence with what has been stated in the introduction to this volume. However, some references to other non-Western countries proved essential, at least when this is crucial to convey the essence of the measure or in light of its chronological development.

Shifting to the second mentioned objective that we pursue in this part of the book, we decided to go beyond 'clusterisation' as just presented. In fact, this part also strives to single out the main legal issues connected to the use of each group of tools and, at the same time, gives an overview of how courts handled the issue. Notably, some of these technologies – for the very reason that they are particularly recent – have not been the object of court rulings yet, at least if one considers the main top courts, such as supranational courts like the European Court of Justice and the European Court of Human Rights as well as domestic supreme and constitutional courts. Nonetheless, some principles have been elaborated by judges in previous cases, dealing more generally with technology and security, and they may work as guidance, applicable to these forms of advanced technologies. In these cases, we recall such principles and explain how they can be applied to novel and most advanced tools.

It is relevant to point out that, in this part, we pursue the two mentioned purposes in parallel. This means that, in enucleating and describing each category of technology (according to the four clusters anticipated above), we discuss at the same time arising legal issues, in light of courts' case law where possible. Indeed, these two dimensions, i.e., the technical and the legal one, are inextricably intertwined, although the legal aspects naturally tend to develop at a later stage than the technical ones.

As in Part I, also at the end of Part II, we decided to provide an Appendix that synthesises our typology of counter-terrorist uses of technology.

At this point, we can start with the first category, i.e., technologies aimed at identifying and assessing risks, and its related legal issues.

3. Identifying the threat: surveillance through the collection and retention of metadata

Starting in chronological order, we can now analyse the form of surveillance performed through the collection of metadata, which evolved from a very traditional method to the use of tools grounded on artificial intelligence algorithms.

As a preventive surveillance measure, the scanning of communication patterns is normally done by taking into consideration only metadata, and not the content of the communication. Metadata is a collection of 'descriptive'[1] information concerning the communication itself: from IP addresses to the length of the communication and the locations of the users, etc. The common trait of metadata is that it is *about* the communication.[2] Before delving into legal issues of metadata collection, a short introductory note on how it works can be useful to fully grasp its functioning.

1. TECHNICAL FUNCTIONING OF METADATA SURVEILLANCE

From a technical viewpoint, metadata collection does not entail, per se, any particularly advanced technological apparatus; it is enough that, first, there is an act legally obliging communication service providers

[1] United Nations Office on Drugs and Crime, Surveillance and Interception of Communications https://www.unodc.org/e4j/zh/terrorism/module-12/key-issues/surveillance-and-interception.html accessed 31 July 2024.

[2] Nora Ni Loideain, 'EU Law and Mass Internet Metadata Surveillance in the Post-Snowden Era' (2015) 3 Critical Analysis and Current Challenges 53.

to keep this data; and, second, that public authorities have the possibility to access it, when this is necessary. In some cases, data is automatically accessed; in other circumstances, a request is needed. From what has been said, the cooperation between public authorities and private entities, meaning communication service providers, is essential. Public-private cooperation will be a recurring topic in our analysis of the use of technology in counter-terrorism and, as we will see in the conclusions of this volume, it may cause significant issues from a legal perspective.

Staying focused on the functioning of metadata surveillance, it underwent an evolution, from more traditional techniques, explained above and only requiring access to data, which was then analysed manually or with the help of traditional software, to more advanced ones. These advanced mechanisms often require the use of intelligent algorithms. Specifically, algorithms based on artificial intelligence may prove helpful when metadata is crossed in order to profile the users of communication technology.[3] Profiling is a procedure originally performed by providers – so, by private entities – for mere commercial purposes, in order to get people's preferences and direct their marketing strategies.

After the 9/11 attacks, the benefits of profiling in the fight against crime quickly emerged. Therefore, public authorities began to make use of profiling tools or rely on profiling made by private bodies. Profiling means matching available information about an individual in order to categorise people into groups, analyse, and, to some extent, predict their behavior. When profiling is done through metadata, it enhances the informative value of the metadata itself. By matching a set of information that, per se, does not reveal much about an individual, it is possible to gain much more knowledge about their preferences, habits, choices, etc. In this way, their behavior can be predicted, including dangerous or potentially risky acts.

Advanced technology – in the form of artificial intelligence – is mainly relevant when such prediction is concerned. Intelligent algorithms are able to divide or classify people into different groups, then grade their 'risk level', and to do so in an extremely rapid manner. Afterwards, these algorithms have the capacity to build a sort of 'ranking' of the risk that users of communication services may endanger security by engaging

[3] Arianna Vedaschi, 'Privacy and data protection versus national security in transnational flights: the EU–Canada PNR agreement' (2018) 8 IDPL 124.

in criminal (especially terrorist) activities. These operations take place not only quickly but also automatically, and without any human involvement, something that can have different legal consequences (see *infra*).

2. LEGAL DEVELOPMENT AND ISSUES OF METADATA SURVEILLANCE

2.1 The United States as the 'Pioneer' of Metadata Surveillance

In a diachronic perspective, significant interest in the retention of metadata as a national security tool was first shown by the United States.[4] The fact that the United States was the absolute forerunner of metadata surveillance is due to two main factors. The first is a factual, contingent factor: as known, the United States was the first country, in 2001, to suffer from the destructive consequences of a major jihadist attack. Consequently, they were urged to put in place countermeasures much more quickly and urgently than other countries. The second factor, instead, is a legal one: the US legal culture and, consequently, its legal framework is less permeated – compared to the European one – with privacy and data protection concerns. Despite privacy having its roots in the United States,[5] in this legal environment, it developed as a right that could frequently be overridden by other interests, especially by national security. Such a feature made it smoother for US public authorities to compel communication service providers to retain metadata based on counter-terrorism legislation. In this regard, the first relevant piece of legislation was the USA PATRIOT Act 2001[6] (hereinafter, the Patriot

[4] David D. Cole and James X. Dempey, *Terrorism and the Constitution: Sacrificing Civil Liberties in the Name of National Security* (NYU Press 2002).

[5] On the origins of a right to privacy in the United States, reference is to Samuel Warren and Louis Brandeis, 'The Right to Privacy' (1890) 4 Harv LR 193. The conception has evolved through the years. David D. Cole and Federico Fabbrini, 'Bridging the Transatlantic Divide? The United States, the European Union, and the Protection of Privacy Across Borders' (2016) 14 Intl J Const L 220.

[6] Uniting and Strengthening America by Providing Appropriate Tools Required to Intercept and Obstruct Terrorism Act of 2001, P.L. 107–56, 115 Stat. 272.

Act), the most well-known omnibus anti-terrorism law ever passed by the US Congress. Section 215 of the Patriot Act[7] required all communication providers to collect all metadata and make it immediately available to governmental entities (without distinction). The letter of the law provides that collection can be performed only insofar as it is 'relevant to an authorised investigation'. Notwithstanding its literal drafting, this provision has been consistently interpreted to mean that the general need to prevent terrorism threats and to guarantee national security is enough to authorise federal authorities to conduct such a program. Therefore, it practically applies to any US citizen, without distinguishing whether or not he/she is under investigation.

Moreover, Section 215 contained a sunset clause,[8] so this norm originated as a temporary provision. However, any time Section 215 came to its expiry date, it was repeatedly extended until nowadays.[9] From a general comparative perspective, it should be noted that this practice, consisting of placing a sunset clause on particularly controversial counter-terrorism measures and then regularly extending it, often without appropriate guarantees in terms of parliamentary procedure, is very common in the comparative scenario[10] and leads to the *de facto* normalisation of emergency legislation.[11] With specific focus on Section 215 of the Patriot Act, after the latest extension, in 2015 its content was incorporated – with some amendments that we will explain immediately *infra*

---

[7] Michael J. Woods, 'Counterintelligence and Access to Transactional Records: A Practical History of USA Patriot Act Section 215' (2005) Journal of National Security Law and Policy 37.

[8] On sunset clauses and their use, among others, in emergency legislation, Antonios Kourotakis, *The Constitutional Value of Sunset Clauses: An Historical and Normative Analysis* (Routledge 2017).

[9] Christopher A. Donesa, 'Is "Secret Law" Really Either? Congressional Intent, Legislative Process, and Section 215 of the USA PATRIOT Act' (2015) 3 National Security Law Journal 101.

[10] Chiara Graziani, *Sicurezza e diritti in tempi di terrorismo internazionale. Tra endiadi e antitesi* (Editoriale scientifica 2022) 147.

[11] The phenomenon of the normalisation of emergency has been widely studied by Italian scholars. Giuseppe de Vergottini, *Nuovi conflitti e sfide della democrazia* (Il Mulino 2004); Arianna Vedaschi, À la guerre comme à la guerre*? La disciplina della guerra nel diritto costituzionale comparato* (Giappichelli 2007)183.

– in the USA Freedom Act 2015.[12] Hence, metadata surveillance became, not only *de facto*, but even *de jure* permanent in the United States. The mentioned amendments brought by the USA Freedom Act to the content of Section 215 of the Patriot Act consisted of formally setting a narrower authority for governmental access to metadata. In particular, it required that the government ask telephone and internet companies to disclose metadata, while, under the original drafting of Section 215, the latter was stored and automatically sent to governmental entities. Although this formal request seems to be an improvement, it must be remarked that the government still retains wide discretion as to the selection of the circumstances and people whose metadata is needed. In other words, the government could request metadata even of those people who are not suspected.

Therefore, the current US framework regarding metadata retention results in a particularly intrusive regime, raising significant Fourth Amendment concerns. As known, the Fourth Amendment is the constitutional clause from which privacy rights can be inferred in the US legal system.[13] It prohibits 'searches and seizures' unless authorised by a warrant issued 'upon probable cause'. The described metadata collection and retention framework appears to be patently incompatible with this provision. Nevertheless, when the retention programme set up by the Freedom Act was challenged before courts, the government repeatedly justified it in light of the third-party doctrine, according to which users cannot expect confidentiality of data they voluntarily disclosed to a third party (in this circumstance, communication service providers).[14] This approach, however, started to be put into question in 2018, when the federal Supreme Court, in *Carpenter v. United States*,[15] ruled that the third-party doctrine does not automatically apply when surveillance is carried out through advanced technology, which allows the collection

---

[12] H.R. 2048, Pub. L. 114–23.

[13] Samuel Warren and Louis Brandeis, *op. cit.*

[14] Katz v. United States, 389 US 347 (1967); United States v. Miller, 425 US 435 (1976); Smith v. Maryland, 442 US 735 (1979). Richard A. Epstein, 'Privacy and the Third Hand: Lessons from the Common Law and Reasonable Expectations' (2009) 24 Berkeley Technology LJ 1199.

[15] 138 S. Ct. 2206 (2018). See Mary-Kathryn Takeuchi, 'A New Third-Party Doctrine: The Telephone Metadata Programme and Carpenter v. United States' (2019) 94 Notre Dame LR 2243.

of a much wider set of data than the one originally made available to third parties. This sort of 'multiplier effect' of the amount of data is due to the increasing capacity of technology tools to profile people, retrieving a significant amount of information on them. Indeed, the *Carpenter* decision did not address specifically metadata retention, being focused on a different issue, i.e., GPS (Global Positioning System) localisation for law enforcement purposes. Nevertheless, the rationale expressed therein constituted a significant breakthrough, potentially applicable to metadata retention through advanced algorithms. While the Supreme Court has not had a chance yet to rule on the metadata provisions of the USA Freedom Act, lower courts have had the chance to address and adjudicate the issue of metadata retention with reference to the previous rules, i.e., those set by Section 215 of the Patriot Act (so, before the changes brought by the USA Freedom Act). The most well-known case in this regard is *United States v. Moalin*.[16] With this decision, delivered in 2020, the US Court of Appeals for the Ninth Circuit held that Section 215 of the Patriot Act violated the Fourth Amendment. By recalling *Carpenter*, the judges ruled that the information available to public authorities (specifically, the National Security Agency) was much wider – due to profiling algorithms – than information originally given by users to communication service providers. As a result, the third-party doctrine does not apply according to the Court of Appeals. This case law has not had further developments since the decision of the Court of Appeals was not challenged before the Supreme Court. At the same time, the *Moalin* judgment has not had major practical consequences because its object (Section 215 of the Patriot Act) was no longer in effect. Nevertheless, at least theoretically, it might be considered as a glimpse toward some better standards of protection of privacy rights, in case the same approach is adopted in potentially forthcoming cases regarding the new data collection regime (based on the USA Freedom Act). It must be said that a real turning point would come if the Supreme Court embraced similar stances, something that seems unlikely, if one considers that in a recent case, namely *Fazaga*,[17] it refrained from reviewing the merits of the applied surveillance program, alleged by the plaintiffs to be discriminatory against the Muslim community. The Supreme Court motivated its decision by affirming that

[16] United States v. Moalin, No. 13–50572 (9th Cir. 2020).

[17] Federal Bureau of Investigation v. Fazaga, 595 US 344 (2022).

the review would have interfered with State secrecy, which legitimately shields the details of surveillance measures.

2.2 The 'Migration' of Metadata Surveillance to Europe

At the end of this overview of the US context, it is necessary to shift to Europe. The European landscape originally differed from the US one as far as data retention is concerned, insofar as this practice was not immediately resorted to after the 9/11 events as a national security tool. However, over the years, the situation changed, and we could notice a certain convergence with the US data retention regime.[18] Again, there is a factual and a legal explanation for the slower introduction of data retention in Europe. From the factual viewpoint, the dangers of the terrorism threat were not perceived in Europe as strongly as in the United States, at least at the very beginning (i.e., in the aftermath of the 2001 events) and until 2004 and 2005 when terrorism directly targeted Europe, with the attacks in Madrid and London, respectively. From the legal perspective, then, Europe is traditionally more observant of privacy and data protection safeguards, which makes the enactment of surveillance legislation more cautious. However, after 2004–2005, privacy and data protection concerns were partially set aside in favour of national security, and the need to enact data retention legislation was perceived at the European level as well. Consequently, the institutions of the then-European Community passed Directive 2006/24/EC[19] (the so-called data retention directive). The data retention directive called on Member States to oblige communication service providers to retain all metadata for a time lapse between 6 and 24 months and make this data available to (undefined) domestic authorities at their request. As known, the data retention directive was completely invalidated by the European Court of Justice

[18] David D. Cole and Federico Fabbrini, *op. cit.*

[19] Directive 2006/24/EC of the European Parliament and of the Council of 15 March 2006 on the retention of data generated or processed in connection with the provision of publicly available electronic communications services or of public communications networks and amending Directive 2002/58/EC, OJ L 105, 13.4.2006,

(ECJ) in 2014 with the *Digital Rights Ireland* decision,[20] due to concerns related to privacy, data protection and the principle of proportionality.[21] In brief, the ECJ found at least four major flaws in the directive. First, it did not provide Member States with criteria to select the retention period between the very wide span of 6–24 months. Second, it did not clarify whether the domestic authorities enabled to access metadata had to be a judicial or at least an independent administrative one. Third, it did not provide for any form of oversight, aimed at checking whether access to metadata respected basic data protection guarantees. Fourth, it did not prescribe appropriate remedies in case collection and use of metadata was performed in violation of any norms.

Given the ECJ's ruling, some domestic norms implementing the directive were either declared unconstitutional or repealed, while other countries did not bring significant changes, practically depriving the ECJ's decision of its effects.[22] The natural consequence was that significant fragmentation arose at the national level, given that, still at present, the EU has abstained from adopting a new regulatory framework on the retention of metadata. At the same time, the current EU rules on data protection – Regulation (EU) 2016/679[23] and Directive (EU) 2016/680,[24]

[20] Judgment of the Court (Grand Chamber), 8 April 2014, *Digital Rights Ireland Ltd v. Minister for Communications, Marine and Natural Resources and Others and Kärntner Landesregierung and Others*, Joined Cases C-293/12 and C-594/12.

[21] Arianna Vedaschi and Valerio Lubello, 'Data Retention and its Implications for the Fundamental Right to Privacy. A European Perspective' (2015) 10 Tilburg LR 14; Elspeth Guild and Sergio Carrera, 'The Political and Judicial Life of Metadata: Digital Rights Ireland and the Trail of the Data Retention Directive', CEPS Paper, 29 May 2014 https://www.ceps.eu/ceps-publications/political-and-judicial-life-metadata-digital-rights-ireland-and-trail-data-retention/ accessed 31 July 2024.

[22] Marek Zubik, Jan Podkowiki and Robert Rybski (eds), *European Constitutional Courts towards Data Retention Laws* (Springer 2021).

[23] Regulation (EU) 2016/679 of the European Parliament and of the Council of 27 April 2016 on the protection of natural persons with regard to the processing of personal data and on the free movement of such data, and repealing Directive 95/46/EC (General Data Protection Regulation), OJ L 119, 4.5.2016.

[24] Directive (EU) 2016/680 of the European Parliament and of the Council of 27 April 2016 on the protection of natural persons with regard to

also known as the General Data Protection Regulation and the Data Protection Law Enforcement Directive, respectively – do not give any specific guidance on the matter, being limited to posing general principles of privacy law that could be analogically extended.

The mentioned fragmentation is evident if one considers that Member States apply very different rules on key features regarding metadata retention. A 2020 report of the Council of Europe[25] conducted a very large survey – surveying not only EU countries but also those countries outside of the EU – and pointed out that all EU Member States (including the United Kingdom, which, at that time, had not left the EU yet) have an active domestic data retention regime and that these frameworks vary as to three main issues. The first issue is the length of the retention, going from very long periods, such as the 6 years in Italy, to much shorter ones, such as the 1-year rule in Belgium. The second is authorities that can access the data. In some countries – the majority, indeed – jurisdictional authorities are vested with this power. There are still some other jurisdictions where this task is left in the hands of administrative bodies or even intelligence forces. There are examples, among others, in Spain, where intelligence can file a request of access that service providers must fulfill, and in Denmark, where access can be requested by 'administrative authorities' without further specification. The third is the type of remedy that can be resorted to in case metadata is illegally processed,[26] which is fully judicial in some cases, as in France, while entrusted to administrative authorities in others; the United Kingdom is an example.

Although the *Digital Rights Ireland* ruling, mentioned above, was a landmark one, it did not deeply address the use of advanced technology. The reason for this lack of specific reference to technology is evident if

---

the processing of personal data by competent authorities for the purposes of the prevention, investigation, detection or prosecution of criminal offences or the execution of criminal penalties, and on the free movement of such data, and repealing Council Framework Decision 2008/977/JHA, OJ L 119, 4.5.2016.

[25] Giorgi Jokhadze, 'Data Retention in the States Parties to the Budapest Convention on Cybercrime', Survey Report 2020, Council of Europe https://rm.coe.int/2088-32-data-retention-report-2020/1680a1f305 accessed 31 July 2024.

[26] The term 'processing' includes any form of collection and use of data aimed at producing information useful for a certain purpose.

one considers that the decision was delivered in 2014, when technology tools existed and were used, even if they were not as advanced as they are nowadays. Rather, a clarification over the use of advanced technology for metadata surveillance purposes came from the ECJ in 2020, when the Court adjudicated two 'twin cases', *La Quadrature du Net*[27] and *Privacy International*.[28] In deciding on these preliminary references raised by French and Belgian judges (*La Quadrature du Net*, joining the two cases), on the one hand, and by a UK tribunal (*Privacy International*) on the other hand, the Court addressed the issue of automated analysis of metadata collected for the prevention of terrorism.[29] More specifically, the referring judges asked the Court to determine whether EU law prevented Member States from enacting domestic pieces of legislation – as those in force in their jurisdictions – that allowed real-time collection of metadata and its analysis by intelligent algorithms. Real-time collection means that metadata is available to public authorities as soon as it is collected by the provider, without any kind of request; this metadata is then automatically analysed, meaning that an algorithm identifies categories of users and assigns a level of risk to them. The ECJ did not deny that this system can be useful for the purposes of crime prevention, especially terrorism, but the judges placed several caveats on the possibility to use it: for instance, it must be for a limited period of time and subject to effective review by a court or independent administrative authority issuing binding decisions. If these cautions are correctly implemented, automated analysis can be an effective and perfectly lawful tool to fight against terrorism. In doing so, the ECJ confirmed an approach that was already visible in *Digital Rights Ireland*, as well as in other cases related to the balance between privacy and national security,[30]

---

27 Judgment of the Court (Grand Chamber) of 6 October 2020, *La Quadrature du Net and Others v. Premier Ministre and Others*, Joined Cases C-511/18, C-512/18 and C-520/18.

28 Judgment of the Court (Grand Chamber) of 6 October 2020, P*rivacy International v. Secretary of State for Foreign and Commonwealth Affairs and Others,* Case C-623/17.

29 Valsamis Mitsilegas, Elspeth Guild, Elif Kuskonmaz and Niovi Vavoula, 'Data Retention and the Future of Large-scale Surveillance: The Evolution and Contestation of Judicial Benchmarks' (2022) 29 Eur LJ 176.

30 Reference is to some landmark cases: Judgment of the Court (Grand Chamber) of 6 October 2015, *Maximillian Schrems v. Data Protection Commissioner*, Case C-362/14 (*Schrems I*); Judgment of the Court (Grand

where, although not with specific reference to the retention of metadata, the Court addressed the use of (more or less advanced) technology in the fight against terrorism.

The stance is shared by the European Court of Human Rights (ECtHR) that, in examining the UK regime of metadata surveillance,[31] ruled in 2021 that metadata surveillance does not breach privacy and free speech rights per se, insofar as sufficient guarantees in terms of *ex ante* oversight and *ex post* review are ensured, something that the UK regime under decision did not do. Reference is to *Big Brother v United Kingdom*, which can be considered as a full-fledged *summa* of the previous ECtHR's case law on privacy and data protection guarantees in the field of security.

In sum, despite the fact that putting everyone of us under surveillance undoubtedly impacts the principle of presumption of innocence, European supranational courts have accepted these measures as necessary tools to foster effective counter-terrorism action, and they have done so even when artificial intelligence is involved. This attitude might illustrate the increasing need to *perceive* security, which has characterised civil society since the outbreak of a threat, such as international terrorism, whose main features are unpredictability and lack of a constant strategy. As a matter of fact, public authorities around the world have frequently leveraged people's search for *perception* of security, enacting measures that made them *feel* safe – something that does not automatically result in an increase in *real* security.

Chamber) of 16 July 2020, *Data Protection Commissioner v Facebook Ireland Limited and Maximillian Schrems*, Case C-311/18 (*Schrems* II).

[31] European Court of Human Rights (Grand Chamber), *Big Brother Watch and Others v. the United Kingdom* (apps nos. 58170/13, 62322/14, 24960/15), 25 May 2021.

4. Identifying the threat by scanning the web: the flagging and removal of terrorist content

On the same line addressed previously, i.e., the need to make people feel safe by identifying potential security threats, another essential tool was developed: the use of algorithms to flag terrorist content online. Through searching for potentially radicalising content, the perception that the web is a 'safe place' may rise. In addition, this is a way to try to prevent terrorist content from materialising into terrorist acts.

As far as this strategy is concerned, it consists of scanning the web to check whether terrorist materials are posted online; a distinction is necessary. Technology tools – and algorithms in particular – are used both to *flag* terrorist content and to *remove* such materials. These two different types of actions are part of the 'content moderation' task of web platforms, usually regulated by their terms of service. In order to flag certain content as terrorist, and then even remove it, the algorithm needs to *assess* the risk that such content is dangerous, using criteria that it has 'learned' thanks to the training received when it has been programmed. When applying the criteria, the algorithm does so in an autonomous way, i.e., building its own reasoning to perform the assessment of the terrorist risk embodied in the scanned content.[1]

This scanning activity, performed by algorithms, implies that web platforms are fathomed, resulting in full-fledged surveillance. When compared to other types of surveillance led by public authorities, this is a type of surveillance where private bodies (internet platforms) also

[1] Alessia Zornetta and Ilka Pohland, 'Legal and Technical Trade-Offs in the Content Moderation of Terrorist Live-Streaming' (2022) 30 Intl J of Law and Information Technology 302; Stuart Macdonald, Sara Giro Correia and Amy-Louise Watkin, 'Regulating Terrorist Content on Social Media: Automation and the Rule of Law' (2019) 15 Intl J of Law in Context 183.

play an important role, as will be clearer in the next pages. From a legal viewpoint, this key role of private entities has crucial implications, which we will highlight when relevant, in the remainder of the book.

Before examining the legal regulation (and sometimes the lack thereof) of terrorist content moderation, we found it useful to provide, at first, an overview of how algorithms used in this context work, in order to then focus on legal aspects with such a background in mind.

1. TECHNICAL FUNCTIONING OF TERRORIST CONTENT FLAGGING AND REMOVAL

From a strictly technical viewpoint – which, as hinted, is crucial to fully analyse legal developments and issues – algorithms can be used in several ways to scan the web and detect potentially dangerous content. Without analysing each technical detail in-depth, we can nonetheless give an overview of the main techniques.[2] Importantly, such an overview does not concern any specific legal system; rather, the aim is just to give a general idea of how these algorithms can *technically* work. We will focus later on (whether and) how these technical features are regulated.

Delving into the technical functioning of flagging algorithms, it is possible to list at least four main macro-categories of these artificial intelligence tools: natural language processing; image matching; clustering; recidivism tackling.

The first category, i.e., natural language processing,[3] consists of algorithms that are 'fed' with writings (statements, messages, articles, etc.) that have been largely acknowledged to convey terrorist ideas. In this way, the algorithm 'learns' how to recognise 'dangerous' words or syntagms and point them out.

There are three main applications of natural language processing to the identification of terrorist contents.

---

[2] For an analysis, see Chiara Graziani, 'Terrorismo internazionale, radicalizzazione e tecnologia' (2023) Federalismi.it 56.

[3] Javier Torregrosa, Gema Bello-Orgaz, Eugenio Martínez-Cámara, Javier Del Ser and David Camacho, 'A Survey on Extremism Analysis Using Natural Language Processing: Definitions, Literature Review, Trends and Challenges' (2023) 14 Journal of Ambient Intelligence and Humanized Computing 9869.

The first application is called 'lexical or vectorial based analysis'. Through this type of analysis, the algorithm represents the texts available on the web as a set of 'tokens'. Each token is made up of the aggregation of groups of words to which a percentage of risk is assigned, depending on the words used, how they are combined together, etc. Just to give an example, the word 'jihadism' per se can be attached a high percentage of risk if used together with other qualified words (e.g., 'war', 'faith', etc.), but its risk percentage can decrease when it is introduced in an educational or academic context. This is something that the algorithm can recognise if words are placed together with others that convey such a context (e.g., 'lecture', 'class', 'exam', etc.). This is an attempt – which is being constantly refined and improved – to enable the algorithm to consider the context of a message, rather than the mere sequence of words.

The second way to apply natural language processing to the identification of terrorist content is 'neural language modelling'. Similar to the previous one, this technique aims to consider the context as much as possible. Based on neural language modelling, the algorithm is trained to recognise the correlations that exist between words. Neural language modelling algorithms differ from those based on lexical or vectorial analysis because they can learn to recognise and assess the risk of words that had not been previously introduced as input and/or in different languages. In other words, their learning performance is very high, so they are particularly advanced algorithms.

The third method grounded on natural language processing is the syntactic and/or semantic feature analysis. Pursuant to this technique, algorithms can detect the 'emotional value' of certain statements or messages. By 'emotional value' we mean the sentiment that is conveyed by a message (happiness, sadness, anger, grievance, etc.). These algorithms, classified as 'sentiment analysis tools',[4] are very advanced in detecting the signs of certain emotions, even if they are still far from perfection in their interpretation as indicators of a specific state of mind or intention. Consequently, they are subject to significant percentages of mistakes and misinterpretation. Indeed, the sentiment conveyed by a statement can be misunderstood even by a human operator, so it is particularly complex to

---

[4] Shakeel Ahmad, Muhammad Zubair Asghar, Fahad M. Alotaibi and Irfanullah Awan, 'Detection and Classification of Social Media-Based Extremist Affiliations Using Sentiment Analysis Techniques' (2019) 9 Human-centric Computing and Information Sciences 1.

develop algorithms that 'never fail' in this specific field, notwithstanding all the remarkable technical advancements.

The second macro-category of techniques that we mentioned is image matching.[5] It was developed insofar as the web is not limited to hosting merely written contents: millions of photos, videos, and other non-written content are posted every day. Image matching consists of feeding the algorithm with images that represent, directly or indirectly, terrorist content. In this way, the input 'teaches' the algorithm how terrorist photos or videos appear, and the algorithm is able to recognise their basic features when they are displayed online. Image matching algorithms improve and become increasingly more refined thanks to experience: the higher the number of images they are fed with, the more able they will become to recognise terrorist photos and videos, even if they significantly differ from the 'model' they have been taught.

The third macro-category is made up of clustering algorithms.[6] These tools work by grouping items that have similar features. For instance, they group and analyse social media accounts of people who have been convicted of terrorist offences and extract their main characteristics. Relevant elements can be: liking certain webpages or content; having certain accounts among their network; re-posting some specific content; and so on. Clustering algorithms are able to compare these characteristics to those of other accounts that exist online, and rate their likelihood of being 'terrorist' accounts. If such a likelihood is high, the account is flagged and eventually removed.

The fourth and last macro-category is that of so-called recidivism tackling algorithms. These algorithms are able to assess whether new accounts that subscribe to a platform are likely to be 'fake' accounts, replicating others that have already been removed (by the platform itself

---

[5] David García-Retuerta, Álvaro Bartolomé, Pablo Chamoso and Juan Manuel Corchado, 'Counter-Terrorism Video Analysis Using Hash-Based Algorithms' (2019) Algorithms 110; Majid KhosraviNik and Mohammedwesam Amer, 'Social Media and Terrorism Discourse: The Islamic State's (IS) Social Media Discursive Content and Practices' in Majid KhosraviNik (ed), *Social Media Critical Discourse Studies* (Routledge 2023) 124.

[6] Gian Maria Campedelli, Iain Cruickshank and Kathleen M. Carley, 'A Complex Networks Approach to Find Latent Clusters of Terrorist Groups' (2019) 59 Applied Network Science 1.

or by public authorities) because they posted terrorist content. For this reason, they can also be referred to as 'repeat offenders algorithms'.[7] They work by combining some of the techniques addressed above. For instance, they may either resort to image matching to check whether a post is similar or identical to a previous one uploaded by a user whose account has been removed, or they may compare the disabled account to a certain cluster and measure their level of risk.

All these techniques are under continuous development and update and are massively employed by ICT companies, often without precisely disclosing them to their users. These two factors (quick development and lack of transparency from the side of platforms) make it very complex to frame a detailed regulation of these mechanisms, as will be made clear from the remainder of the analysis.

2. LEGAL DEVELOPMENT AND ISSUES OF TERRORIST CONTENT FLAGGING AND REMOVAL

The terrorist content on the web became an increasingly serious issue as soon as the internet started to spread as a common tool, available to most individuals without excessive costs and efforts. As a matter of fact, the wide use of the web allows terrorists, on the one hand, to radicalise others, and it permits potential adepts, on the other hand, to be easy prey to radicalisation strategies. As a consequence, there has been no doubt that radicalisation needs to be fought, especially in its online forms, as offline radicalisation still represents an existing, yet not so pressing, issue. Coherently, if one looks at the comparative scenario, there is a proliferation of pieces of legislation criminalising or enacting measures against the terrorist use of the internet. Giving a full set of examples of these norms would not be feasible and, most of all, would fall outside the aim of the present work; nonetheless, it is possible to recall the main tools.

---

[7] Alec MacMillen, 'Can an Algorithm Identify Repeat Offenders?' (2019) Chicago Policy Review (Online) 1. See also Valentine Crosset and Benoît Dupont, 'Cognitive Assemblages: The Entangled Nature of Algorithmic Content Moderation' (2022) 9 Big Data & Society 1.

2.1 The European Scenario: Attempts at Regulation

From the European Union side, the main relevant legal sources are the following: Directive (EU) 2017/541,[8] according to which 'Member States shall take the necessary measures to ensure that the distribution, or otherwise making available by any means, whether *online* or offline, of a message to the public'[9] related to terrorism; Regulation (EU) 2021/784,[10] titled 'on addressing the dissemination of terrorist content online'; Regulation (EU) 2022/2065[11] (so-called Digital Services Act), which is more general – i.e., not focused on terrorism – and this does not exclude repercussions on the fight against online terrorist content, insofar as it mandates digital platforms to perform risk assessments of their contents and publish transparency reports on the removal of posts. Another EU rule which is not directly referred to terrorism, but has important repercussions, is the liability regime set by Article 14 of Directive 2000/31/EC[12] (so-called E-Commerce Directive). According to this source, internet service providers are not liable for the content hosted by their platforms as long as they are not (and could not have been) aware of the presence of illegal material. The same approach was confirmed by the Digital Services Act (DSA), at Article 6, according to which there is no liability for the provider who 'does not have actual knowledge of illegal activity or illegal content and, as regards claims for damages, is not aware of facts or circumstances from which the illegal activity or illegal

---

[8] Directive (EU) 2017/541 of the European Parliament and of the Council of 15 March 2017 on combating terrorism and replacing Council Framework Decision 2002/475/JHA and amending Council Decision 2005/671/JHA, OJ L 88, 31.3.2017.

[9] Ibid., art. 5 (emphasis added).

[10] Regulation (EU) 2021/784 of the European Parliament and of the Council of 29 April 2021 on addressing the dissemination of terrorist content online, OJ L 172, 17.5.2021.

[11] Regulation (EU) 2022/2065 of the European Parliament and of the Council of 19 October 2022 on a Single Market for Digital Services and amending Directive 2000/31/EC (Digital Services Act), OJ L 277, 27.10.2022.

[12] Directive 2000/31/EC of the European Parliament and of the Council of 8 June 2000 on certain legal aspects of information society services, in particular electronic commerce, in the Internal Market ('Directive on electronic commerce'), OJ L 178, 17.7.2000.

content is apparent; or [...] upon obtaining such knowledge or awareness, acts expeditiously to remove or to disable access to the illegal content.' Interestingly, the concept of awareness is clarified by Recital 53 of the Digital Services Act, based on which a provider is *de jure* considered to be aware of certain content when this content has been reported and its illegality is patent, without any need for an in-depth review.[13] Patent illegality is very likely with *some* terrorist content, while others, as pointed out before, are much more nuanced.

Furthermore, there are laws and regulations that Member States adopted to implement EU norms (in the case of a directive) or adapt their own domestic legal orders to them (in the case of a regulation) or, in some cases, that they issued even before the EU stepped in. It is the case, among others, of Germany.[14]

Putting together the rules arising from these EU law sources – along with domestic pieces of legislation arising from or in connection to them – the framework is very blurred concerning the specific area of the resort to technology to flag terrorist messages. Looking at these acts – especially Regulation (EU) 2021/784 – they are quite detailed regarding the rules of transparency and accountability to be complied with and the procedures to remove dangerous contents,[15] but they do not provide any precise rules on which type of technology should be used, how algorithms should be framed, and to what extent automation is reliable. Although, on one side, this can be understood in light of the rapid change of technologies, on the other, it creates a relevant lacuna. Moreover, from the viewpoint of legal responsibility, the scenario is not so clear in the EU. As said, there is no full liability of providers for the content they

[13] Florence G'Sell, 'The Supreme Court of the United States Dismisses the Liability of Social Media Platforms for Hosting Terrorist Content', *SciencesPo, Chair Digital, Governance and Sovereignty*, 20 May 2023 https://www.sciencespo.fr/public/chaire-numerique/en/2023/05/20/supreme-court-rules-on-liability-for-terrorist-content/ accessed 31 July 2024.

[14] Netzwerkdurchsetzungsgesetz (NetzDG) 1. September 2017 (BGBl. I S. 3352).

[15] Specifically, Regulation (EU) 2021/784 provides (art. 7) that platforms 'shall set out clearly in their terms and conditions their policy for addressing the dissemination of terrorist content, including, where appropriate, a meaningful explanation of the functioning of specific measures, including, where applicable, the use of automated tools' and deliver annual transparency reports on their content moderation activity.

host, but they can nonetheless be held liable when they know – or should have known – about the illegality of certain material, something that is not always straightforward to determine. In addition, Regulation (EU) 2021/784 provides for economic penalties for those providers that do not promptly remove content when ordered to do so by a public authority, comply with their own terms and conditions on the removal of terrorist content, or fail to respect some transparency and reporting obligations.[16] Although these penalties cannot be considered a full-fledged form of responsibility, they still constitute a restraint which *de facto* obliges platforms to exercise stronger control over their content and, more generally, their moderation activity. This recent feature has contributed to making the overall picture more blurred.

Through this framework, if we can say that at least the EU took steps to make legal systems uniform, we should remember that there is another player that, although being a crucial one, is not bound by such legal rules. The reference is to the United Kingdom (UK). As widely known, after Brexit the UK is no longer a Member State of the European Union and is consequently not obliged to respect EU law. Thus, the UK passed its own provisions regarding the removal of terrorist content online, namely the Online Safety Act 2023.[17] This act is a piece of legislation that aims at making the UK 'the safest place in the world to be online'.[18] The Online Safety Act, although it provides rules for online platforms that are very similar to those laid down by Regulation (EU) 2021/784 and Regulation (EU) 2022/2065, has some additional constraints for platforms. For instance, similarly to what Regulation (EU) 2021/784 does, the UK legal framework obliges online platforms to comply with

[16] Regulation (EU) 2021/784, art. 18.

[17] Online Safety Act 2023, ch. 50.

[18] UK Government, Department for Science, Innovation and Technology and The Rt Hon Michelle Donelan, 'Overwhelming Support for Online Safety Act as Rules Making UK the Safest Place in the World to be Online Become Law', 27 October 2023 https://www.gov.uk/government/news/overwhelming-support-for-online-safety-act-as-rules-making-uk-the-safest-place-in-the-world-to-be-online-become-law#:~:text=News%20story-,Overwhelming%20support%20for%20Online%20Safety%20Act%20as%20rules%20making%20UK,over%20what%20they%20see%20online accessed 31 July 2024.

removal orders coming from a public authority (so-called notice and take down),[19] while at the same time proactively monitoring the web to spot and remove clearly illegal content (terrorism, child-pornography, etc.). In this regard, the UK legal tool explicitly refers to platforms using algorithms, including machine learning, for this purpose, while in the EU framework there is a more generic reference to 'automation' as a possible tool to enhance the application of policies aimed at countering terrorist speech. Although this divergence may seem a mere matter of wording, it makes a difference from a legal angle, as the UK framework legally acknowledges – and to some extent legitimises – the daily practice of platforms consisting of massive resort to intelligent automation.

2.2 The 'Liberal' Approach of the United States

Moving to the other side of the Atlantic, i.e., looking at the United States, the scenario is partially different from the European one. In the United States, due to the traditional interpretation of the First Amendment as an (almost) absolute right, pieces of legislation explicitly criminalising – or anyway punishing – online terrorist speech face a more arduous path to be passed. Consequently, from the US perspective, those who disseminate terrorist content on the internet can be prosecuted only insofar as their posts or messages amount to other crimes, such as material support to terrorism[20] (even extensively interpreted). From the viewpoint of platforms, instead, Section 230 of the Communications Decency Act (CDA) practically grants them full immunity from any accountability for the content they host, stating that '[n]o provider or user of an interactive

---

[19] According to Regulation (EU) 2021/784, the competent authority is a public body, identified by each Member State, that is in charge of issuing removal orders, i.e., ordering the platform to eliminate content that the competent authority itself has assessed as potentially dangerous. EU law does not give guidelines as to whether this authority should be a judicial or administrative one. Hence, some Member States even chose police bodies (e.g., Denmark). For an analysis of the EU regulation and the regime it establishes, see Tarik Gherbaoui and Martin Scheinin, 'A Dual Challenge to Human Rights Law: Online Terrorist Content and Governmental Orders to Remove It' (2023) European Journal of Human Rights 3.

[20] 18 U.S.C. § 2339B. On the interpretation of this norm, see James J. Ward, 'The Root of All Evil: Expanding Criminal Liability for Providing Material Support to Terror' (2008) 84 Notre Dame L Rev 471.

computer service shall be treated as the publisher or speaker of any information provided by another information content provider'.[21]

Differently from the EU scenario, in the United States providers can never be held liable, not even where they were aware of the presence of illegal content on their online space. In the EU, conversely, platforms are immune only as long as they did not know and, importantly, as long as they do not qualify as 'publishers'. On the other hand, the US regime is a full-fledged shield that online platforms enjoy when they operate in the US scenario, as web platforms are never considered 'publishers' bearing responsibility for the content they host.

The mentioned CDA, containing this very wide form of immunity, was enacted in 1996, well before the current breakthroughs of the internet and the digitalisation of almost any human activity. Hence, it would be quite obvious to think of an amendment to update this framework, given the huge developments of the digital environment. However, at least at the federal level, so far, it is still the cornerstone of the liability regime in the United States since there are no further specific pieces of legislation regulating the conduct of online platforms concerning the content they host, and so Section 230 CDA remains the only legal source on the topic.

Nevertheless, several proposals are currently lying before Congress,[22] some of them radically suggesting the repeal of Section 230 CDA, while others are aimed at limiting the immunity of platforms by making them liable when the content is patently illegal (e.g. direct incitement to terrorism, child pornography, etc.). At this point, none of these reform projects has become law yet.

Besides, it must be said that such a reform of internet platforms' liability regime is certainly not driven by the case law of US courts, which are generally still very convinced about the need for full immunity of platforms.

---

[21] Section 230, Communications Decency Act, 47 U.S.C. § 230 (1996).

[22] See Congressional Research Service, 'Section 230: An Overview', 4 January 2024 https://crsreports.congress.gov/product/pdf/R/R46751#:~:text=Section%20230%20of%20the%20Communications,users%20of%20interactive%20computer%20services accessed 31 July 2024. See, e.g., the Kids Online Safety Act and the EARN IT (Eliminating Abusive and Rampant Neglect of Interactive Technologies) Act.

Focussing on the case law, US courts ruled several times on Section 230 CDA in cases where the plaintiffs alleged that some social media platforms should have been held responsible/accountable for contributing to the radicalisation of people who then participated in the organisation and/or perpetration of terrorist attacks damaging the plaintiffs themselves or their relatives. For instance, we can refer to two landmark cases, *Force v. Facebook* (2019)[23] and *González v. Google* (2021),[24] where the District Court for the Second Circuit held that Section 230 barred the plaintiffs' arguments and found that there was no civil liability on Facebook nor on Google due to the fact that their algorithms favoured the finding of radicalising content by their users. Only a dissenting opinion by Justice Katzman, issued in *Force v. Facebook*, partially diverged, drawing attention to the algorithm's capacity to influence users' searches. Justice Katzman stated that '[m]ounting evidence suggests that providers designed their algorithms to drive users toward content and people the users agreed with – and that they have done it too well, nudging susceptible souls ever further down dark paths'.[25] Nonetheless, this remained a dissenting opinion without – so far – specific practical consequences.

The rulings in *Force* and *González* were confirmed in second instance. The judicial path of both cases proceeded before the United States Supreme Court. In 2020, the federal supreme jurisdiction did not grant certiorari in *Force v. Facebook*, thus refusing to examine the issue. The Court, instead, granted certiorari in *González v. Google*. When it agreed to decide *González*, at the same time the Supreme Court accepted to review another case, *Twitter v. Taamneh*, which had some similarities, along with differences, with *González*. Notwithstanding the differences – which we are going to explain – *Taamneh* affected the way in which *González* was decided. In *Twitter v. Taamneh*, Twitter was accused of having 'aided and abetted' terrorism in suggesting, through its algorithms, radicalising content to some users who had then taken part in a terrorist attack. Therefore, the claim was not based only on Section 230 CDA; it was grounded on Section 2333 of the Antiterrorism and Effective Death Penalty Act[26] too. The 'aiding and abetting' provision

---

[23] 934 F.3d 53, 84 (2d Cir. 2019).

[24] 2 F.4th 871 (9th Cir. 2021).

[25] Force v. Facebook, 934 F.3d 53, 84 (2d Cir. 2019), Katzman J., dissenting.

[26] 18 U.S.C. § 2333.

implies criminal responsibility (and not civil liability, as in Section 230 CDA), and was the only issue to be addressed by US courts, who refrained from ruling on Section 230.

In *Twitter v. Taamneh*, both the first instance court and the Court of Appeals for the 9th Circuit[27] had stated that there was a causal link between recommendations made by Twitter's algorithm and the radicalisation of the users who then took part in terrorist acts, and this could give rise to criminal liability. However, in 2023, the Supreme Court[28] reversed the decision of the Court of Appeals and held that the allegations were insufficient to establish whether or not Twitter aided and abetted terrorism.

In synthesis, although having granted certiorari, the Supreme Court decided 'not to decide.' What is interesting is that the same Court, when addressing the *González* case,[29] remanded it back to the lower court, asking it to reconsider the allegation in light of the *Taamneh* ruling. And the court did so notwithstanding the fact that *Taamneh* was indeed not decided on the merits (but merely on a lack of allegations) and that it was addressed from the perspective of criminal (and not civil) responsibility, since the judges chose not to examine Section 230 of the CDA in a separate part of their reasoning. In doing so, it is quite evident that the Supreme Court preferred not to take an explicit stance on the matter, perceived as a 'pivotal topic'. The approach of the Supreme Court shows a clear will to keep the *status quo* in the field of social media and other platforms' liability for how their algorithms work and suggest content, without taking any direct position on it. Anyway, the case has not come to an end, since, while writing this manuscript, the lower court has not decided the *González* case yet.

This quite conservative approach was confirmed in July 2024, when the US Supreme Court decided the *Moody v. Netchoice* case.[30] In this judgment, the supreme justices of the United States held that two state laws adopted by Florida and Texas, which imposed some limits on the irresponsibility of platforms, might violate the First Amendment, and asked the lower court to reconsider the merits to assess whether they should actually be found unconstitutional. Although the Supreme Court

---

[27] Taamneh v. Twitter, No. 18–17192.

[28] Twitter v. Taamneh, 598 US 471 (2023).

[29] González v. Google, 598 US 617 (2023).

[30] Moody v. NetChoice, 603 US 707 (2020).

did not declare the unconstitutionality, there are some signs guiding the Court of Appeal's decision towards such a declaration. For instance, the Supreme Court held that, even in the sensitive activity of content moderation, platforms shall enjoy the widest possible protection arising from the First Amendment.

The attitude of US courts – especially the Supreme Court – is likely to have crucial consequences.

First, it is undoubtedly influencing the political sphere. It is not by chance that no legislative step has been taken yet at the federal level on this topic; the posture of the US Supreme Court is unquestionably a significant hurdle in this regard.

The second consequence is that the approach of the Supreme Court, especially in *Moody v. Netchoice*, is very likely to influence pending or forthcoming judicial cases involving (or potentially involving) state laws trying to stem the extreme lack of liability established in favour of providers. In fact, future judicial cases are not unlikely, since, in spite of the federal level's inertia to reform the immunity of providers for contents they host, only in 2023, state legislatures introduced 144 measures to regulate the moderation of online content, and others had been introduced in earlier years.[31] These 'safety laws' are actually more focused on children's online safety than specifically on the flagging and/or removal of terrorist content; nevertheless, in the concept of 'protection of children', it is possible to embed also the need to keep them away from terrorist material, given that children and teenagers are considered vulnerable groups, particularly prone to the risk of radicalisation.

In addition to norms regulating how content should be moderated on the web, several US states are also passing laws imposing transparency requirements on platforms. This is the case of California, which enacted Assembly Bill No. 587 (known as AB587) in September 2023. AB587 obliges online platforms to disclose their content moderation policies. In other words, platforms are expected to clarify how they use algorithms, what they define as 'dangerous content', and actions taken to eliminate these materials. This law, which shows considerable similarities with EU legislation on transparency addressed above, was challenged by X (Twitter) in September 2023 on the ground that it breaches the First

---

[31] National Conference of State Legislature, Social Media and Children 2024 Legislation https://www.ncsl.org/technology-and-communication/social-media-and-children-2024-legislation accessed 31 July 2024.

Amendment. According to X's lawyers, AB587 'pressure[s] social media platforms to "eliminate" certain constitutionally-protected content viewed by the state as problematic'.[32] The case has already been decided in the first instance by Judge William Shubb[33] of the US District Court for the Eastern District of California. In December 2023, he rejected X's claim and ruled that the state of California had justifiable reasons to request transparency from platforms, so the provision does not amount to an 'unjustified or unduly burdensome' requirement 'within the context of First Amendment law'. The judgment has been appealed, but no second instance ruling has been issued yet while writing this volume. Nonetheless, given the outcome of *Moody v. Netchoice*, the answer – in case this litigation reaches the Supreme Court – might be an easy forecast, since the stance in the latter case appears a total win for platforms.

On a partially different note, the fact that Californian law – similarly to other US state pieces of legislation and the EU framework – imposes transparency requirements on platforms about their policy leads us to address another relevant aspect, i.e., that such platforms effectively enjoy a very high rate of discretion as to the framing of such policies. And, what is more, if not compelled to, they often do not release much information about them. As a matter of fact, notwithstanding domestic pieces of legislation, there are several areas in which they still retain significant freedom of choice. For instance, they are able to decide how to combine the algorithmic techniques addressed above to build their own automated systems to identify content and assess the danger it poses; they can determine to take down content based on their own decision (so-called proactive measures), without waiting for an order from a public authority; in doing so, they follow their own assessment of what is 'dangerous' material. Additionally, there are platforms (e.g., Meta) that have established their own 'boards' to hear complaints from users alleging that their material has been removed without posing any concrete risk.

This panorama shows how relevant the interference of private powers has become in the three traditional functions coinciding with State

---

32 Lou Kettering, 'Elon Musk's X Corp. Challenges California Law Requiring Social Media Companies to Publish Content Moderation Policies', *JuristNews*, 10 September 2023 https://www.jurist.org/news/2023/09/elon-musks-x-corp-challenges-california-law-that-requires-social-media-companies-publish-content-moderation-policies/ accessed 31 July 2024.

33 X Corp. v. Bonta, 2:23-cv-01939 WBS AC (E.D. Cal. Dec. 28, 2023).

powers: the legislative function, in determining what terrorism is; the executive function, in practically enforcing this definition; and even the judiciary one, in establishing bodies – whose guarantees of independence are doubtful – tasked with hearing complaints. The rise of these 'private powers' in this field, embodying 'para-legislative', 'para-executive', and 'para-judiciary' functions is self-evident and concerns the globe as a whole. The enhancement of private bodies and an increasingly tight partnership – and sometimes even something more – with public authorities constitutes one of the recurring features in all the uses of technology as a counter-terrorism tool. Despite partially different features than the ones we have observed with regard to terrorist content online, the intrusiveness of private powers will be evident also in the next topic we address, that is the use of biometry to identify the terrorist threat.

5. Identifying the threat by relying on biometric data

The use of biometry to scan potential threats to national security is another tool that has been applied massively, i.e., without distinction between those who are suspected of posing a threat to national security and those who, instead, belong to 'ordinary citizens'. Again, despite being a powerful tool to assess the risk of terrorism, it may infringe upon the basic principle of presumption of innocence; at the same time, it could generate a so-called chilling effect, negatively impacting rights such as freedom of expression and freedom of assembly.[1]

Biometric data can be defined as information concerning the unique characteristics of the human being. By saying 'unique' we mean those characteristics that differentiate each human being from all the others, or in other terms, traits that none of us share with any other person. Within the category of biometric data fall facial images, fingerprints, iris, and voice. Facial images and fingerprints are undoubtedly the most used, at least for public security aims. In this regard, it is relevant to point out that, especially with facial recognition, consent stops being an essential

[1] Monika Zalnieriute, 'From Data Retention to Facial Recognition Technologies: Counter-Terrorism Implications for Human Rights and the Rule of Law', *Submission to Thematic Report for the United Nations General Assembly 76*, June 2021. The problem of the chilling effect has been highlighted also by the European Court of Human Rights in the decision *Glukhin v. Russia* (app. no. 1519/20), 4 July 2023. Although this judgment involves a respondent state, i.e. Russia, where standards of democracy are much lower than in the contexts that we analyse in this book, the issue is thoroughly analysed by the Court of Strasbourg, with considerations that can be applied also to other legal systems.

ground for the collection of data, as facial images are mostly collected without people knowing about it.[2]

Before digging into the technical functioning of the use of biometric data and, subsequently, its legal regulation and main issues raised in Western advanced democracies, it is necessary to point out that the origins of these techniques do not trace back to the Western side of the world, but rather to the East. Without any doubt, the 'champions' of biometrics for security purposes are Asian countries, most notably South Korea and, even if not comparable under the viewpoint of democratic standards, China.[3] It has been reported that China has been relying on biometric data – most of all, facial images – to check people present in public spaces since at least 2018, thanks to the so-called smart glasses technology, with which Chinese police have been endowed since that time.[4] Smart glasses, also called surveillance glasses, are wearable computers, taking the form of ordinary glasses, that enable the user – in this case, police personnel – to take real-time photos of people and immediately compare them to governmental databases containing images of suspected and convicted criminals. In turn, it has been reported that, starting from 2019, the South Korean government financed the Artificial Intelligence and Tracking System Construction Project, under which private companies are allowed to collect biometric data of people and share it in secret (i.e., without the consent of the data subject) with governmental authorities in order to advance immigration screening and check public events.[5]

With the breakout of the Covid-19 pandemic, biometric technologies were further enhanced, as Asian countries – China and South Korea are, again, examples – started using them to track the virus and its contagion.[6] Although it is undeniable that, in this case, biometrics were used for public

---

[2] Evan Selinger and Woodrow Hartzdog, 'The Inconsentability of Facial Surveillance' (2020) 66 Loyola LR 53.

[3] Yan Luo and Rui Guo, 'Facial Recognition in China: Current Status, Comparative Approach, and the Road Ahead' (2021) 25 U Pa J L & Soc Change 153.

[4] BBC, Chinese Police Spot Suspects with Surveillance Sunglasses, 7 February 2018 https://www.bbc.com/news/world-asia-china-42973456 accessed 31 July 2024.

[5] Chris Lott, 'Korean Facial Recognition Project Faces Opposition', *Hackaday*, 1 December 2021.

[6] Arianna Vedaschi, 'General Report', in Id (ed), *Governmental Policies to Fight Pandemic. The Boundaries of Legitimate Limitations on Fundamental Freedoms* (Brill 2024).

health rather than for public security purposes, this phenomenon encouraged further studies and so biometric tools became even more refined.

These techniques were developed at first in the Eastern world due to the different conception of privacy and data protection in these areas, yet they quickly spread to the West. Just to give some data, a recent report by the United Nations Counter-Terrorism Executive Directorate (CTED)[7] showed that, as of the end of 2021, 118 out of 193 Member States of the United Nations have implemented biometric surveillance systems for counter-terrorism purposes, almost all of them relying on artificial intelligence algorithms. In Figure 5.1, the CTED displayed the trends of using these mechanisms in each geographic area.

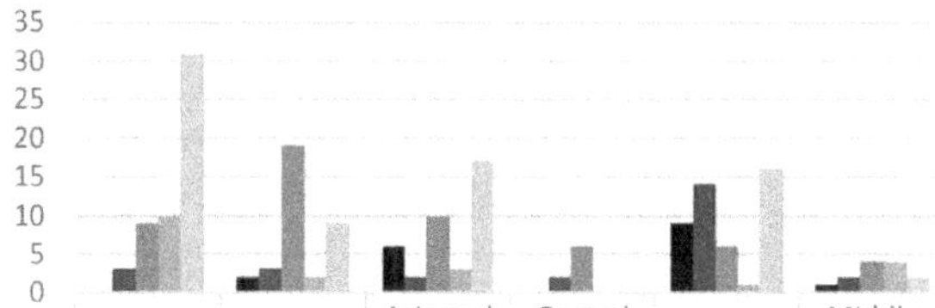

	Africa	Americas	Asia and Pacific	Central Asia	Europe	Middle East
Yes	0	2	6	0	9	1
Largely	3	3	2	2	14	2
Partially	9	19	10	6	6	4
Marginally	10	2	3	0	1	4
No/ Insufficient information	31	9	17	0	16	2

Source: UN CTED, CTED Analytical Brief: Biometrics and Counter-Terrorism 2021 https://www.un.org/securitycouncil/ctc/sites/www.un.org.securitycouncil.ctc/files/files/documents/2021/Dec/cted_analytical_brief_biometrics_0.pdf.

Figure 5.1 *Biometric recognition across the world*

After this brief overview, we can now focus on how facial recognition algorithms work in practice, so as to then concentrate on the legal issues.

[7] United Nations Counter-Terrorism Executive Directorate, 'CTED Analytical Brief: Biometrics and Counter-Terrorism', 2021 https://www.un.org/securitycouncil/ctc/content/cted-analytical-brief-biometrics-and-counter-terrorism accessed 31 July 2024.

1. TECHNICAL FUNCTIONING OF THE USE OF BIOMETRIC DATA FOR SECURITY PURPOSES

The ways in which intelligent algorithms can be combined with biometric data and work for the sake of public security are multifold. Indeed, the technical procedures are the same in the case of biometric recognition employed for other, less sensitive aims (let us just think, among others, of when we use our facial image to unlock our smartphones). It is useful to give some of these technical notions about these systems, insofar as they will help better understand their applications and, where present, their legal regulation.

First of all, biometrics can be used both for verification and for identification,[8] and both verification and identification are useful in the field of public security. When used for verification, it means that a specific facial image – or another piece of information pertaining to the category of biometrics, such as, e.g., a fingerprint – is compared to another specific facial image – and/or other biometric data – in order to verify whether or not they belong to the same person. An example could be when, at the airport, a facial recognition system scans one person and compares him/her to the photo displayed on his/her passport, to assess whether the analysed person and the legitimate owner of such passport coincide. Differently, identification is when the image (or other data) is collected and compared not to another specific image, but to a whole database (e.g., those databases owned by law enforcement authorities and containing the data of offenders). Let us imagine a large event where, to access the venue, people have to undergo a facial scan to make sure that none of those who enter the event coincides with pre-identified criminals whose facial image is contained in police databases.

Given the purpose of this section, we focus on identification techniques, widely used in counter-terrorism and, more generally, in the fight against crime; nevertheless, it must be noted that they work much like

---

[8] Michael O'Flaherty, 'Facial Recognition Technology and Fundamental Rights' (2020) 6 EDPL 170; European Union Agency for Fundamental Rights (FRA), 'Facial Recognition Technology: Fundamental Rights Considerations in the Context of Law Enforcement', 27 November 2019 https://fra.europa.eu/en/publication/2019/facial-recognition-technology-fundamental-rights-considerations-context-law accessed 31 July 2024.

verification, the only difference being the term of comparison, i.e., a specific image for verification, a whole database for identification.

Additionally, biometric recognition can be carried out through 'live' or 'non-live' technologies. Using live biometrics means that the operation of comparison between the collected and the stored data takes place immediately and always without the individual being aware. What are also immediate are the consequences. To be clearer in this regard, let us imagine that a person's facial image is collected by public authorities, immediately matched with a database of terrorists, and recognised as one of those terrorists. At this point, public authorities might be entitled, based on the applicable law, to arrest him/her or apply other coercive measures. Being a very risky situation in terms of respect for human rights – since the application of the recognition algorithm and its possible mistakes are not verified – it is normally only allowed for very serious crimes, and terrorism falls among these crimes.

Coming to the more technical side, what the algorithm does when trained to work as a biometric system is, first of all, to scan, measure, and take note of the relevant features of the concerned person. More specifically, it will, for example, measure the distance between all parts of the face and produce a pattern thereof.

These measuring operations take place in an extremely short time span, less than one second, and, immediately afterward, the algorithm is able to communicate with the matching database and recognise whether or not that unique biometric pattern can be found in the database as well. At this point, the human operator (e.g., the policeman) will perform an action based on the output, for instance arresting or questioning the person in case he/she has been recognised as a terrorist present in the matching database. In this context, it represents the functioning of facial recognition mechanisms and showing a *modus operandi* applicable also to other biometric-based systems.

Still, from a merely technical viewpoint, technical studies have been conducted on possible mistakes that may happen with biometric systems.[9] In this regard, it is useful to differentiate between the recognition of face, fingerprint, iris, and voice.

---

[9] Ramandeep Chahal, 'A Comparative Study of Various Biometric Approaches' (2017) 4 International Journal of Engineering Applied Sciences and Technology 30; Joy Buolamwini and Timnit Gebru 'Gender Shades: Intersectional Accuracy Disparities in Commercial Gender Classification'

Starting with faces, the most common mistakes that have been identified have to do with the position of the face and the color of the person's skin. In fact, it has been noticed that, on one side, different face positions may make facial features more difficult to match; on the other, people with black skin are usually more easily conflated with others due to the technical functioning of the algorithm.

Fingerprints are the most traditional biometric features to be scanned and analysed. Being the most 'ancient' ones, they can be easily cheated, for instance by employing artificial fingers; moreover, fingerprint recognition systems do not work well in cases of cuts and marks on a person's finger.

Moving to irises, it has been demonstrated that mistakes may originate from particular lighting effects or reflective surfaces, which do not allow precise scanning, and so a precise matching, of the iris.

The recognition of the voice has a major drawback, i.e., external noises. In the case of noises coming from the outside, the system may perform poorly.

It is crucial to emphasise again that these possible mistakes that we have just mentioned are technical, so they are connected with how the recognition algorithm works; for this reason, they can be called 'technical biases'. They do not have to do with 'human biases', i.e., the result of human ideologies or prejudices that might be incorporated in algorithms. Yet, human biases may represent a significant risk as well. Let us think of a facial recognition system that has been trained only – or mainly – based on facial features of people from a certain area of the world, showing similar traits. This algorithm will, of course become more efficient in recognising people of such origin and so have a bias towards them.[10] Both technical and human biases can raise significant legal issues, which will be discussed next.

(2018) 81 Proceedings of the 1st Conference on Fairness, Accountability and Transparency 77; Giuseppe Mobilio, 'Your Face is Not New to Me – Regulating the Surveillance Power of Facial Recognition Technologies' (2022) 12 Internet Policy Review 1.

[10] On the biases that can be introduced by human beings in facial recognition systems, see Joy Buolamwini, *Unmasking AI. My Mission to Protect What is Human in a World of Machines* (Penguin Books 2023).

2. LEGAL DEVELOPMENT AND ISSUES OF USE OF BIOMETRIC DATA FOR SECURITY PURPOSES

In order to get to the core of legal issues raised by biometric tools, it is essential to clarify how different legal systems employ them in their security practice, so categorising the possible ways of using these systems to guarantee security. As said several times throughout this volume, we mainly focus on advanced Western democracies; nonetheless, we must be aware that even wider uses are made in countries based on a different legal tradition, such as the Asian one.[11]

To give a taxonomy of the possible methods to use biometric recognition technologies as public security tools, one of the most interesting criteria is the purposes for which they are used. From this perspective, we can detect three main contexts corresponding to three different, but partially related, aims: immigration and border security; public spaces; and the identification and prosecution of single individuals suspected of terrorism. There is a major difference among the first two contexts and the third one, meaning the first two imply *massive* application of biometric surveillance to each and every person, while the third consists of individual measures and, consequently, is less problematic from the perspective of human rights because it has a lower impact – if compared to the other two – on the principle of the presumption of innocence and, thus, on the rule of law. Therefore, we will mostly focus on biometric surveillance in the field of immigration/border control and in public spaces. As in previously analysed measures, it can be useful to address separately the context of the United States from Europe, where European Union law merges and interacts with the legislation of Member States. References to New Zealand and Australia are present as well, insofar as they serve as useful comparators in this field.

2.1 Immigration and Border Control

Beginning with immigration and border control, biometric scanning is highly developed in advanced Western democracies. However, before

[11] Peter Dauvergne, 'Facial Recognition Technology for Policing and Surveillance in the Global South: A Call for Bans' (2022) 43 Third World Quarterly 2325.

digging into European and US regulation, it is interesting to look at (whether and) how the matter is regulated at the international and supranational levels, which should always steer State legislation and practice in security matters with a global reach.

2.1.1 The international framework

Taking steps from the international layer, as it often happens with national security strategies implying high reliance on technology, regulation on that point is relatively scarce. Looking at the United Nations (UN) framework, the first clear references to the use of biometrics in counter-terrorism are found in two resolutions of the Security Council: Resolution 2322(2016)[12] and Resolution 2396(2017).[13] Within these two legal tools, biometric surveillance is regarded as a way to manage border security, but if one reads their provisions, they are extremely vague. As a matter of fact, the 2016 resolution just calls on Member States to share information, including biometric data, about terrorists and suspected terrorists. The one adopted in 2017 is relatively more specific than its predecessor since it calls on national authorities to implement systems for the collection of biometric data, so, at least, it invites action. Importantly, the provision on biometrics in Resolution 2396(2017) was adopted under Chapter VII of the UN Charter,[14] so it is legally binding on Member States (which, as already pointed out, mostly intervened to implement the call coming from international actors), while it was a mere non-legally binding recommendation in Resolution 2322(2016). It is not by chance that both these resolutions were enacted in the years when the phenomenon of so-called foreign terrorist fighters (FTFs) was particularly widespread and represented a serious concern for international and domestic institutions. In fact, the FTF issue implied stronger attention to the international dimension of the struggle against terrorism, which was

---

[12] United Nations Security Council, S/RES/2322(2016).

[13] United Nations Security Council, S/RES/2396(2017).

[14] On this topic, see Krisztina Huszti-Orbán and Fionnuala Ní Aoláin, 'Use of Biometric Data to Identify Terrorists: Best Practice or Risky Business?', Human Rights Center, University of Minnesota (2020) https://www.ohchr.org/sites/default/files/Documents/Issues/Terrorism/biometrics-report.pdf accessed 31 July 2024; Katja Lindskov Jacobsen, 'Biometric Data Flows and Unintended Consequences of Counterterrorism' (2021) 103 Intl Rev Red Cross 619, 638.

perceived as a problem 'of the Western side of the world' as well. In these circumstances, the use and exchange of biometric data was deemed an undoubtedly efficient way to enhance international measures implying cooperation among states.

From the international level, we can now shift to lower levels of government, i.e., the supranational and the domestic ones. It seems appropriate to begin with Europe rather than with the United States. Actually, EU law offers a supranational framework as well as several widespread guidelines in this regard, and the domestic dimension is highly influenced by it, while the United States is not steered by a supranational framework.

2.1.2 The 'European side'

Starting from the most 'old-style' application of biometric recognition, i.e., border security management, the European Union has started using biometric data at the borders within the Common European Asylum System (CEAS). The main and most ancient reference in this regard is the Eurodac system, which entered into force in 2003[15] and then, after ten years, was replaced by Regulation (EU) 2013/603.[16] Eurodac allows for the collection of fingerprints (i.e., biometric data) of all those who seek asylum; all fingerprints are gathered in a database (the Eurodac database), which can be accessed by Europol and by national police forces when they are investigating some serious crimes, including terrorism.[17]

[15] Council Regulation (EC) No 2725/2000 of 11 December 2000 concerning the establishment of 'Eurodac' for the comparison of fingerprints for the effective application of the Dublin Convention, OJ L 316, 15.12.2000.

[16] Regulation (EU) No 603/2013 of the European Parliament and of the Council of 26 June 2013 on the establishment of 'Eurodac' for the comparison of fingerprints for the effective application of Regulation (EU) No 604/2013 establishing the criteria and mechanisms for determining the Member State responsible for examining an application for international protection lodged in one of the Member States by a third-country national or a stateless person and on requests for the comparison with Eurodac data by Member States' law enforcement authorities and Europol for law enforcement purposes, and amending Regulation (EU) No 1077/2011 establishing a European Agency for the operational management of large-scale IT systems in the area of freedom, security and justice (recast), OJ L 180, 29.06.2013.

[17] Niovi Vavoula, 'Interoperability of EU Information Systems: The Deathblow to the Rights to Privacy and Personal Data Protection of

The possibility for law enforcement authorities to access the Eurodac database was introduced by the 2013 amendment, which entered into force in 2015. Thus, the Eurodac method, in addition to being crucial to facilitate the application of the 'Dublin system' (i.e., a set of criteria that the European Union uses to determine which Member State has to examine individual asylum applications), started to strongly contribute to law enforcement authorities' action in rapidly identifying suspected terrorists.[18] Nevertheless, this new functioning seemed to embody a very serious risk of discrimination, insofar as it may create a bias according to which asylum-seekers – thus, citizens of third countries, coming from outside the European Union, often religiously and culturally distant from EU Member States – are more likely to be engaged in terrorist activities. This would constitute discrimination on the ground of nationality, which is prohibited by EU law, and training any algorithm on (only) Eurodac data is a slippery slope. To reinforce the argument of the risk of discrimination, we can mention the case law of the European Court of Justice. The latter has never had the chance to rule directly and specifically on Eurodac; however, in a case decided in 2006, *Huber v. Germany*,[19] it maintained that databases available to public authorities (in general, not specifically Eurodac) cannot be used for law enforcement purposes unless specifically developed for that aim. Yet, the 'cry' of the Luxembourg Court seems to have remained unheeded, considering that Eurodac, although created as an immigration and asylum database, has been regularly used for investigation and prosecution purposes since at least since 2015.

It is noteworthy that the Eurodac system has been further reformed as a consequence of the 2020 Pact on Asylum and Migration (hereinafter, the Pact).[20] The Pact, presented in September 2020 by the European Commission, aimed at the revision and update of the whole

Third-Country Nationals?' (2020) 26 EPL 131.

[18] Elif Mendos Kuşkonmaz, 'The Eurodac Debate: Is It Blurring the Line Between Asylum and Fight Against Terrorism?' (2013) XLV Annales 79.

[19] Judgment of the Court (Grand Chamber) of 16 December 2008, *Heinz Huber v Bundesrepublik Deutschland*, Case C-524/06. Charlotte Bagger Tranberg, 'Proportionality and Data Protection in the Case Law of the European Court of Justice' (2011) 1 IDPL 239, 242.

[20] Sergio Carrera and Andrew Geddes (eds), *The EU Pact on Migration and Asylum in Light of the United Nations Global Compact on Refugees:*

CEAS, including the Eurodac system. In particular, the new Eurodac regulation,[21] which was published in the Official Journal while this book was being written, has repealed and replaced the 2013 tool. With specific regard to biometry, the new Eurodac legislation allows border control authorities to store not only fingerprints but also facial images of asylum seekers, thus expanding the categories of biometric data to be collected. Moreover, the new Eurodac system has lowered the age of people whose fingerprints and facial images can be collected from 14 years-old to 6 years-old and has simplified the procedures for law enforcement authorities to access the database, thereby making interoperability of databases easier within the whole Union.[22]

Still on the European side yet at the domestic level, it can be said that EU Member States are strongly tied to the EU regime, so there are no significant differences. As a matter of fact, the very purpose of regulations under the architecture of EU law is to make Member States' legislation uniform, so this is coherent with the fact that Eurodac is established by a regulation. Within this uniform framework, some interesting considerations can be provided on the United Kingdom, which was a Member State of the EU when Eurodac was set up and developed, and then leave the European Union while some of its most important innovations were brought into practice, positioning itself as a 'hybrid' case. More in detail, when the United Kingdom formally exited the European Union, i.e. on

International Experiences on Containment and Mobility and their Impacts on Trust and Rights (European University Institute 2021).

[21] Regulation (EU) 2024/1358 of the European Parliament and of the Council of 14 May 2024 on the establishment of 'Eurodac' for the comparison of biometric data in order to effectively apply Regulations (EU) 2024/1351 and (EU) 2024/1350 of the European Parliament and of the Council and Council Directive 2001/55/EC and to identify illegally staying third-country nationals and stateless persons and on requests for the comparison with Eurodac data by Member States' law enforcement authorities and Europol for law enforcement purposes, amending Regulations (EU) 2018/1240 and (EU) 2019/818 of the European Parliament and of the Council and repealing Regulation (EU) No 603/2013 of the European Parliament and of the Council, OJ L 1358, 22.5.2024.

[22] On interoperability of EU databases, see Deirdre Curtin and Filipe Brito Bastos, 'Interoperable Information Sharing and the Five Novel Frontiers of EU Governance' (2020) 26 EPL 59.

31 January 2021 (after the end of the so-called transition period),[23] it ceased being bound by the so-called Dublin system, including Eurodac. Since the loss of a partner like the United Kingdom in the prevention of transnational crime – including terrorism – would have been a heavy defeat for the security of the European Union, the latter immediately strove to find ways to keep the same level of cooperation. They reached an agreement only in 2022, with a decision of the Council[24] allowing, on the one hand, EU authorities to make Eurodac data available to the United Kingdom as long as the United Kingdom makes available its own biometric data, collected at the border, based on a previous declaration made by the UK Prime Minister in 2020. Notably, this framework may need an update after the new Eurodac regulation, in order to cover facial images, which were not addressed previously. Anyway, from a practical viewpoint, the United Kingdom continues collecting and using biometric information at the borders in a way that is totally alike to what they did before Brexit. This approach demonstrates that, as in several other post-Brexit situations, the United Kingdom, although having left the European Union, continues applying totally similar rules. Suffice it to say, in this regard, that after Brexit, the UK amended the so-called UK GDPR,[25] to make sure that the UK legal system almost fully replicated the provisions present in the EU general data protection framework. Something similar happened with the Online Safety Act 2023, recalling the EU regulation on the removal of terrorist content online, and even placing some more constraints on providers.

---

[23] See Alberto-Horst Neidhardt, 'Post-Brexit EU–UK Cooperation on Migration and Asylum: How to Live Apart, Together', European Policy Center Discussion Paper, 20 June 2022 https://www.epc.eu/content/PDF/2022/EU-UK_post_Brexit_DP.pdf accessed 31 July 2024.

[24] Council Decision (EU) 2022/1014 of 17 June 2022 on the position to be taken on behalf of the Union vis-à-vis the United Kingdom of Great Britain and Northern Ireland regarding the determination under Article 540(2) of the Trade and Cooperation Agreement between the European Union and the European Atomic Energy Community, of the one part, and the United Kingdom of Great Britain and Northern Ireland, of the other part, of the date from which personal data relating to DNA profiles and dactyloscopy data as referred to in Articles 530, 531, 534 and 536 of that Agreement may be supplied by Member States to the United Kingdom, OJ L 170, 28.6.2022.

[25] Data Protection Act 2018 c. 12.

2.1.3 The 'US side' and some other useful comparators

Shifting to the United States, the use of biometrics to manage borders is very widespread as well. Indeed, the US Department of Homeland Security had resorted to biometric measures for border control even before 9/11, when the threat of international terrorism 'conventionally' broke out.

To go more in-depth about how biometric identification works, it is worth remembering that, in the United States, the handling of external migration is a competence of the federal government. Thus, federal authorities are the most active in developing some very advanced biometric tools to enhance their work. The US Department of Homeland Security is currently developing the Homeland Advanced Recognition Technology System (HART) to replace the current Automated Biometric Identification System (IDENT).

It is worth analysing IDENT first, in order to identify the main differences that HART, if deployed and enacted, would imply. IDENT was released in 1994 as a fingerprint border control system to identify those who tried to illegally cross the US from both the northern and southern borders. When IDENT entered into function, it was not specifically regulated by any legislative act: Congress simply allocated $27 million in the budget and made this amount available to the then-Immigration and Naturalisation Service (INS).[26] The INS developed IDENT as a system to be applied only to aliens who were found illegally crossing the borders. Nevertheless, in 1996, Congress passed the Illegal Immigration Reform and Immigrant Responsibility Act,[27] whose Section 326 requires IDENT to be applied to any aliens, wherever they were found illegally over US territory. On the one hand, including IDENT in the rules provided by the 1996 Act can be seen as an improvement, insofar as IDENT was eventually provided with a legal basis in federal law. On the other hand, with the 1996 Act, IDENT ceased to be a mere immigration tool and started to become a law enforcement instrument, characterised by the worrying feature of being applicable only to foreigners, with the risk of discriminating against them because of their non-US nationality.

---

[26] A US agency was active until 2003 when most of its functions were shifted to three new bodies: the US Citizenship and Immigration Services, the US Immigration and Customs Enforcement, and the US Customs and Border Protection, all depending on the Department of Homeland Security.

[27] Pub. L. (United States) 104–208.

As said, IDENT was initially set up as a tool based on fingerprints, and its reach was then widened to facial images in 2001, with the US Patriot Act.[28] At the same time, facial recognition is used at US borders through the Simplified Arrival System, which records facial images of all passengers landing and exiting from 53 airports located in the United States as well as from 39 seaports. In this way, US federal authorities have an almost complete overview of biometric data of all those who cross the US borders, be they legal or illegal travelers.[29] On the basis of these systems, they are able to arrest migrants or send them back to their countries, without any kind of judicial warrant.

The 'next step' in the use of biometrics at the borders, as anticipated, would be the use of the HART system. HART is not operational yet, and, like its predecessor, IDENT, it is not being developed under a draft law; rather, it only works 'in practice', i.e., as a tool of the US Department of Homeland Security for which Congress has allocated a budget. A first innovation that HART would bring is the range of biometric data that it would collect: not only fingerprints and facial images, but also iris, voice, and even DNA, which is biometric data *par excellence*, being the carrier of the unique genetic information of each person. The second difference between HART and IDENT is that HART would work as a sort of 'database of databases'. In other words, HART would not be limited to storing biometric data of migrants; it would also aggregate – without any consent from data subjects – biometric data available to any federal agency of the United States (e.g., the Federal Bureau of Investigation), state police forces, and even to foreign governments agreeing to cooperate with the United States in this field.[30] Third, HART would be able to perform social media scanning, meaning that it would compare the facial feature of each person with images available on social media, something that clearly clashes with the privacy rights not only of the concerned person but, more widely, of any social media user. Last but not least, while

[28] Pub. L. (United States) 107–56.

[29] Emmanuel Abraham Perea Jimenez, 'The Fourth Amendment Limits of Facial Recognition at the Border' (2021) 70 Duke LJ 1837.

[30] Mizue Aizeki and Paromita Shah, 'HART Attack: How DHS's Massive Biometrics Database Will Supercharge Surveillance and Threaten Rights' (2022) https://surveillanceresistancelab.org/resources/hart-attack-how-dhss-massive-biometrics-database-will-supercharge-surveillance-and-threaten-rights/ accessed 31 July 2024.

the algorithm behind IDENT is traceable, the one on which HART is grounded is a full-fledged black box, i.e., a type of algorithm whose 'reasoning' cannot be known, with serious impairment of the principle of transparency. HART is being developed by the Department of Homeland Security by relying on two private contractors, Northrop Grumman and Veritas Capital, a feature that confirms the undeniable trend towards an increasingly strong public-private partnership when technology becomes an essential tool in security practice.

It must be noted that the US approach is very similar to that of Canada, Australia, and New Zealand in this regard. In fact, all three make wide use of facial recognition at the borders as a tool to identify people and verify whether they match suspected criminals. Among them, Canada is even considering relying on facial images recorded by smartphones to check the borders. The case of Australia is paradigmatic, where the SmartGate system is implemented. SmartGate is a tool present in major Australian airports that is able to automatically check the passport of all travellers without any human interaction. The biometric data recorded by SmartGate (i.e., the facial features of the travelers) are immediately shared with Australian law enforcement authorities, making them available all over the Australian territory. In New Zealand, a similar system exists and it is called eGate.

In general, although these mechanisms are very efficient in making border checks quicker and smoother, doubts about the 'fate' of biometric data arise, since, as seen, they often become available to other bodies beyond those who collect them, potentially infringing on principles such as consent and purpose limitation.

2.2 Biometrics in Public Spaces: Law Enforcement Activities

Until now, we focused on biometrics used in both 'sides' of the Western world (i.e., Europe and the United States) for immigration and border control purposes, and then frequently 'transferred' to law enforcement authorities. After this analysis, we need to concentrate on the second category of applications of biometric technology that we highlighted when introducing the topic. Reference is made to when law enforcement authorities deploy biometric recognition (facial recognition or other tools) in public or publicly accessible spaces, something that happens often – although not necessarily – in large events. In this way, they scan the population as a whole (or, more precisely, all the people who are in a specific public place at a certain moment).

Following the same order as before, we address the European Union first, and then turn our attention on the United States, always with some reference to other comparators, where such comparison is useful.

2.2.1 The 'European side'

In the European Union, a new piece of legislation was enacted imposing norms that impact, among others, the use of biometrics in publicly accessible spaces for law enforcement purposes. Reference is to the Artificial Intelligence Act (hereinafter, AI Act), which has been definitively published in the Official Journal in July 2024 as Regulation (EU) 2024/1689[31] and will become applicable two years after its publication.[32]

It is not the purpose of this work to provide a comprehensive analysis of the AI Act. Nonetheless, we believe that its impact on law enforcement and other activities aimed at guaranteeing security would not be fully understandable without having a general idea of how this piece of legislation is framed and structured, as well as its basic principles. Consequently, in Table 5.1 we provide a general scheme of the regulation.

Coming to the AI Act's implications on our topic, it is undoubtedly a remarkable attempt, from the European Union, to regulate artificial intelligence and its applications, excluding those in the defence and national security fields. Nonetheless, as it often happens, the European Union managed to regulate *de facto* some measures aimed at protecting national security by approaching them from other angles, such as the prosecution of crime and, more in general, law enforcement. As far as the use of biometrics is concerned, this can be observed by looking at how the new regulation addresses the use of biometric systems in publicly accessible spaces. Regulation (EU) 2024/1689 prohibits the use of real-time facial recognition systems – but also other systems applying biometry – in publicly accessible spaces for law enforcement purposes, unless in a list of specific circumstances. More in detail, law enforcement

---

[31] Regulation (EU) 2024/1689 of the European Parliament and of the Council of 13 June 2024 laying down harmonised rules on artificial intelligence and amending Regulations (EC) No 300/2008, (EU) No 167/2013, (EU) No 168/2013, (EU) 2018/858, (EU) 2018/1139 and (EU) 2019/2144 and Directives 2014/90/EU, (EU) 2016/797 and (EU) 2020/1828 (Artificial Intelligence Act), OJ L 1689, 12.7.2024.

[32] Carlo Casonato, 'Unlocking the Synergy: Artificial Intelligence and (old and new) Human Rights' (2023) BioLaw Journal 233.

Table 5.1 General overview of the AI Act: Regulation (EU) 2024/1689

Topic	Explanation
Scope of application	It applies to all providers based in the EU or whose activity has an impact on EU Member States, EU citizens, or persons located in the Union. Hence, the regulation has a trans-territorial application.
Risk-based approach: AI systems are categorised based on their risk rate	**No risk/Minimal risk:** These systems (e.g., video games, spam filters) are not regulated by EU law. **Limited risk:** These systems (e.g., chatbots like ChatGPT) are subject to limited transparency obligations (e.g., they are obliged to disclose to users that contents are generated by AI). **High risk:** These systems (e.g., those applied to recruitment, granting of loans, and other financial decisions) need to comply with a wide set of obligations in order to circulate in the EU market. Among these obligations are: enabling a risk management system, having a clear data governance framework, and providing technical documentation. **Unacceptable risk:** These systems are prohibited (with some exceptions). Among them are those tools using manipulative or deceptive techniques to distort behaviour and decision-making; social scoring; real-time biometric identification in public places.
New governance of AI	Establishment of an **AI Office** (currently hiring and funded by the EU Commission) tasked with the following: • Monitoring the compliance with the regulation by providers; • Hearing providers' complaints in case they are accused of not complying with the regulation; • Investigating risks associated with AI systems; • Establishment of a **Panel of Experts** to support enforcement activities; • Establishment of an **AI Board** (one representative per Member State) tasked with advising and assisting the EU Commission and Member States' authorities about the application of the regulation.
Sanctions	In case providers violate obligations arising from the regulation, penalties are imposed as a percentage of the company's global annual turnover.

Source: Authors (through Microsoft Word).

authorities can use biometric tools in publicly accessible spaces only to localise or identify a person suspected to have committed a serious crime (among which, terrorism-related offences, defined according to national law); to prevent a *specific* and *present* terrorist threat; to search for victims of some crimes (sexual exploitation, trafficking, abduction).[33] Additionally, law enforcement authorities relying on these systems must register them in an EU database and provide a fundamental rights assessment of their functioning; moreover, they need to obtain authorisation to use these tools by a judicial or independent administrative authority. Only in cases of urgency is it possible to proceed without registering the system nor being authorised. The regulation of real-time biometric systems for law enforcement aims is synthesised in Table 5.2.

Table 5.2 Regulation of real-time biometric systems for law enforcement purposes in the AI Act

Topic	**Explanation**
Definition of real-time biometric systems for law enforcement purposes	Systems that enable law enforcement authorities to carry out the real-time matching of biometric data collected in publicly accessible spaces with a remote database.
General rule	**These systems are prohibited**
Exceptions	• Searching for victims of some listed crimes (abduction, sexual trafficking, sexual exploitation); • Preventing a specific and imminent terrorist threat; • Identifying people suspected of serious crimes (among which are terrorism-related offences).

Source: Authors (through Microsoft Word).

On the one side, the EU regulation restricts national authorities' discretion to use these systems by giving a detailed list of the crimes and circumstances in which they can be employed and by requiring that only specific and imminent terrorist threats legitimise the use of these tools (so, they cannot be resorted to for general prevention purposes); on the

[33] Regulation (EU) 2024/689, art. 5, para (d)(ii).

other side – and this is a common issue of counter-terrorism measures – it leaves to Member States the definition of 'terrorist crimes' as well as the evaluation of whether a terrorist threat is specific and imminent.

In the EU Member States, the regulation of biometric tools used for law enforcement purposes is, as evident, strongly influenced by EU law, not only in terms of the just-mentioned framework, which is not applicable yet, but also the general data protection framework is relevant in this regard (in particular, the General Data Protection Regulation – GDPR).[34] Nonetheless, some Member States deserve to be separately addressed because they had started deploying biometric techniques in law enforcement in advance compared to others (meaning, either before the entry into force of the GDPR or the beginning of the discussion on the AI Act[35]) and worked as 'forerunners'.[36] In this regard, Germany, Italy, and the Netherlands are extremely relevant and deserve to be analysed. Afterwards, it is worth addressing the United Kingdom, which ceased being an EU Member State in between the entry into force of the GDPR and the start of the procedure to adopt the AI Act.

In Germany, trials of facial recognition technologies as law enforcement techniques began in 2019 to identify suspicious behaviour in some train stations. Indeed, some trials had been conducted even a couple of years before, in 2017, during the G20 summit in Hamburg, again to protect public order and security by spotting unlawful behavior. Moreover, several municipalities deployed live facial recognition in 2020. These techniques lacked any legal basis and were declared unlawful by some German lower courts.[37]

---

[34] See Lorenzo Cotino Hueso, 'Reconocimiento Facial Automatizado y Sistemas de Identificación Biométrica bajo la Regulación Superpuesta de Inteligencia Artificial y Protección de Datos' (2023) Derecho público de la inteligencia artificial 347.

[35] The first discussions date back to 2021.

[36] Tambiama Madiega and Hendrik Mildebrath, 'Regulating Facial Recognition in the EU', PE 698.021 – September 2021 https://www.europarl.europa.eu/RegData/etudes/IDAN/2021/698021/EPRS_IDA(2021)698021_EN.pdf accessed 31 July 2024.

[37] See Luca Montag, Rory Mcleod, Lara De Mets, Meghan Gauld, Fraser Rodger, and Mateusz Pełka, 'The Rise and Rise of Biometric Mass Surveillance in the EU. A Legal Analysis of Biometric Mass Surveillance Practices in Germany, the Netherlands, and Poland' (2021) https://edri.org

The lack of a legal basis concerned the Italian system as well. As a matter of fact, the Italian police began experimenting with SARI Real Time in 2019, using it in some selected large public events. SARI was able to immediately compare the facial features of those who took part in those events with the characteristics contained in other police databases and – an aspect never officially confirmed – even with the Eurodac database. The deployment of SARI by the Italian police happened merely *de facto*, since no legal source authorised them to resort to this system. Consequently, in April 2021, the Italian Data Protection Authority released an opinion[38] stating that SARI Real Time should not have been used since it lacked a legal basis and resulted in a form of mass surveillance. In light of this opinion, the Italian Government enacted a decree law (then converted into law by the Houses of Parliament)[39] prohibiting the use of facial recognition systems in public places. The prohibition is effective until 31 December 2025. In any case, given the EU framework, it appears unlikely that such a ban will be lifted at the beginning of 2026.

In the Netherlands, biometric data has been resorted to in public spaces, but this method will need to change after the AI Act becomes applicable. From 2018 onwards, biometric data has been processed thanks to a system called CATCH (Centrale Automatische Technologie voor Herkenning – which can be translated as Central System for Recognition based on Automated Technology). However, as noted by scholars,[40] also in the Dutch system, there is no legal basis for CATCH. Rather, the Dutch police issued a document called 'Police Deployment Framework for Facial Recognition Technology' (the Framework). Yet, the Framework cannot be considered at all a legally binding source, so it cannot work as a proper legal basis.

/wp-content/uploads/2021/11/EDRI_RISE_REPORT.pdf accessed 31 July 2024.

[38] Garante per la Protezione dei Dati Personali (Italy), 'Riconoscimento facciale: SARI Real Time non è conforme alla normativa sulla privacy', 16 April 2021 https://www.garanteprivacy.it/web/guest/home/docweb/-/docweb-display/docweb/9575842 accessed 31 July 2024.

[39] Decree Law no. 51/2023, converted into Law no. 87/2023 (Italy).

[40] Maša Galič and Lonneke Stevens, 'Regulating Police Use of Facial Recognition Technology in the Netherlands: The Complex Interplay between Criminal Procedural Law and Data Protection Law' (2023) 14 New Journal of European Criminal Law 459.

Hence, very similar problems characterise the countries – we have analysed three main cases – where facial recognition in public spaces was experimented with at first. Among these, the lack of a legal basis appears to be the main and most apparent one; but even unclear limits to the applicability of those technologies represent an issue, as it is one of the consequences of the lack of a legal basis. To this end, the AI Act seems to be appropriately working as a legal basis, although significantly restricting the circumstances in which biometric recognition will be used in public spaces to a few cases of imminent terrorist attacks.[41]

As regards the United Kingdom, it will not be legally bound by the EU AI Act, nor will the same Act, having been passed by EU institutions after Brexit, be part of so-called EU retained law.[42] Looking at its practice, the United Kingdom, at the time when it was still an EU Member State, was a pioneer of facial recognition in public spaces, trialling it in large events at least from 2015 onwards. Although domestic courts[43] ruled on these technologies and found at least some aspects of potential incompatibility with the European Convention on Human Rights – incorporated into the UK legal system through the Human Rights Act 1998 – UK public authorities keep using very advanced facial recognition algorithms in public spaces. More in detail, at present these tools can be used to identify suspects of any crime, without any distinction between serious and less serious ones, and this is just a matter of practice, since there is no piece of legislation in the UK allowing law enforcement

---

41 On a general note, however, it should be pointed out that the AI Act does not address immigration specifically, and this could be an easily 'crackable' hole for reintroducing limitless biometric surveillance circumventing its guarantees.

42 On the category of EU retained law, see Catherine Barnard, 'Retained EU Law in the UK Legal Orders: Continuity between the Old and the New', in Adam Łazowski and Adam Cygan (eds), *Research Handbook on Legal Aspects of Brexit* (Edward Elgar 2022) 98.

43 See, e.g., the *Bridge* case. *R (Bridges) v. CCSWP and SSHD* [2019] EWHC 2341 (Admin); *R (Bridges) v. Chief Constable of South Wales Police* [2020] EWCA Civ 1058. Andrea Pin, 'Non esiste la "pallottola d'argento": l'Artificial Face Recognition al vaglio giudiziario per la prima volta' (2019) DPCE Online 3075. See also Id, 'A Novel and Controversial Technology. Artificial Face Recognition, Privacy Protection, and Algorithm Bias in Europe' (2021) 30 Wm & Mary Bill Rts J 291.

bodies to resort to them. According to statistics,[44] only in the first half of December 2023, 10 people were arrested thanks to recognition based on intelligent algorithms, including for minor crimes. Differently from the EU scenario, in the United Kingdom there is no (longer any) supranational framework possibly limiting these technologies. Consequently, while in the previously examined EU countries the AI Act might bring positive consequences in terms of limiting the lack of a legal basis and of a clear list of crimes to which facial recognition can be applied, the same will not happen in the United Kingdom. This is one of the main 'fragmentation effects' coming from Brexit. It remains to be seen whether in the future the United Kingdom – much like it did with the regulation of online terrorist content – will adopt any domestic legislation to 'mimic' the EU one and *de facto* re-harmonise the situation. If not, the UK may act as a considerable driver of standard-lowering in this field, something to be carefully considered in the assessment of Brexit's effect.

2.2.2 The 'US side' and some other useful comparators

Shifting our glance to the US side, facial recognition for law enforcement purposes in public spaces is widely resorted to, both at the federal and state level.[45] We will mainly focus on the application of this system by federal agencies, but some examples from states are interesting as well.

According to recent data,[46] at least six federal law enforcement agencies resort to biometrics in their activities. Among these agencies, we

---

[44] See data presented by Asress Adimi Gikay, 'Facial recognition helps fight serious crime, but for minor UK offences it should be off limits', *The Guardian*, 24 December 2023 https://www.theguardian.com/commentisfree/2023/dec/24/facial-recognition-uk-drivers-licence-police-lineup#:~:text=5%20months%20old-,Facial%20recognition%20helps%20fight%20serious%20crime%2C%20but%20for%20minor%20UK,it%20should%20be%20off%20limits&text=Privacy%20campaigners%20have%20long,deploy%20it%20in%20public%20spaces accessed 31 July 2024.

[45] Mailyn Fidler and Justin (Gus) Hurwitz, 'An Overview of Facial Recognition Technology Regulation in the United States', in Rita Matulionyte and Monika Zalnieriute (eds), *The Cambridge Handbook of Facial Recognition in the Modern State* (CUP 2024) 214.

[46] US Government Accountability Office, 'Facial Recognition Technology: Federal Law Enforcement Agency Efforts Related to Civil Rights and Training', GAO-24–107372, 8 March 2024 https://www.gao.gov/products/gao-24–107372 accessed 31 July 2024.

can mention the Federal Bureau of Investigation (FBI), the US Secret Service (USSS), the Bureau of Tobacco, Firearms and Explosives (BTFE), the Drug Enforcement Administration (DEA), Homeland Security Investigations (HSI), and the US Marshals Service (USMS). Although they have different roles in the US legal system and not all of them directly deal with terrorism as their main task, all of them may have to do with terrorist crimes in some circumstances.

Instead of addressing these agencies and the technology tools one by one as a consecutive list, it seems useful to group and compare them based on their main features.

A first distinction needs to be drawn between those systems that take facial images from specific sources and others that, instead, rely on images taken from the whole web. Starting with the second category, collecting facial images from any web resource is highly challenging in terms of privacy rights, since taking these images means circumventing any form of user's consent, which would ordinarily be necessary for the exploitation of one's personal image. Among the companies involved in this controversial activity of collecting photos, Clearview AI, owning the Clearview software, is the main example. The Clearview software is a facial recognition service that is able to 'learn' from the web, taking and retaining the facial images published on any webpage.[47] It means that, as soon as a photo is visible on the web, Clearview is able to collect it and add it in its database. Of course, this does not happen only with web content published in the US, but anywhere in the world, so Clearview has a global reach and, consequently, it also impacts on non-US citizens. At present, Clearview's database contains more than 30 billion facial images. Among US agencies, Clearview is used by the FBI, the BTFE, the DEA, the HSI, and the USMS. The fact that the tool is in the hands of government agencies does not exclude the patent issues of privacy and consent, highlighted above.

The pervasive use of Clearview may even impact more general principles, beyond single rights and freedoms. For instance, let us think again of the presumption of innocence, often mentioned throughout this analysis. In fact, Clearview takes content from every single internet user,

[47] Camilla Dul, 'Facial Recognition Technology vs Privacy: The Case of Clearview AI' (2022) 3 Queen Mary LJ 1.

without making any distinction based on whether his/her online behaviour is potentially dangerous.[48]

Moreover, being Clearview a market operator, it could have a commercial interest in selling collected data, in the logic of the 'surveillance capitalism'[49] that, however, often sits at odds with rights.

Differently from Clearview, other facial recognition systems do not take their images randomly from the web, since they do so only from selected sources. For instance, Thorn and Marynus Analytics, used by the FBI (in addition to Clearview, indeed), only take images existing in law enforcement archives and concerning specific offenders, such as terrorists and sex traffickers. Systems like these are less impactful on privacy and the presumption of innocence, yet they still may pose legal issues insofar as they can make mistakes that, if not promptly reviewed and corrected, are likely to bring serious consequences for individuals, up to the deprivation of their personal freedom.

Another important distinction to be made among these systems concerns their owners. In clearer terms, some of them are directly owned by the agencies themselves, while others are owned by private corporations that become government contractors. While Thorn and Marynus Analyticus are owned by the agencies, the ownership of Clearview lies in the hands of the homonymous US corporation, AI Clearview. This aspect is very significant if one considers how many agencies (see above) rely, exclusively or among others, on the Clearview software. Ownership of the facial recognition system has relevant legal consequences. For example, if the software is owned by a federal agency so, ultimately, by the government – its functioning can be more straightforwardly challenged before courts, insofar as its action could be more easily reconducted to that of the agency; things are more complicated if the owner of the software is a government contractor, since the terms of the contract

[48] In this regard, Clearview was declared illegal in 2021 by the Canadian data protection authority (the Privacy Commissioner) because it allows a form of unlimited bulk surveillance. Office of the Privacy Commissioner of Canada, 'Clearview AI Ordered to Comply with Recommendations to Stop Collecting, Sharing Images', 14 December 2021 https://www.priv.gc.ca/en/opc-news/news-and-announcements/2021/an_211214/ accessed 31 July 2024.

[49] Shoshana Zuboff, *The Age of Surveillance Capitalism: The Fight for a Human Future at the New Frontier of Power* (Public Affairs 2019).

between it and the government may not be totally disclosed, and this may have consequences on the bearing of responsibility. At least theoretically, public ownership should result in better monitoring of the functioning of these systems and, as a consequence, higher rights protection standards. On the contrary, when the software – and thereby the algorithm is owned by private enterprises, as AI Clearview is, this enterprise is grounded on market considerations. For instance, it is well-known that AI Clearview, besides providing governmental entities with its services, also works for other private companies, selling them their services (e.g., it has been reported[50] that it helps some casinos identify their best clients through the photos they own, in order to reward them with incentives). Henceforth, there is a potentially dangerous blend between private and public (or, at least, publicly relevant) activities.

AI Clearview, which is used not only in the US but worldwide, either by public or private bodies, has been widely criticised by scholars and commentators and, in some cases, declared illegal by courts. At this point, a short comparative overview is necessary.

Starting from the United States, several cases have been raised before the courts by human rights organisations, such as the American Civil Liberties Union (ACLU). Actually, these cases ended with settlement agreements, in an extra-judicial manner. For example, in June 2022, ACLU obtained assurances from Clearview AI that it will stop selling facial images to private companies in the United States.[51] The settlement ended judicial litigation that had been initiated before the competent court in Illinois. Although the settlement represents a win in practical terms and in the short run, because Clearview is at least barred from making commercial use of facial images, in the long run and from a general viewpoint, the situation may stand differently. The most serious drawback of having had the issue extra-judicially settled is that this discourages further litigation, and thus the possibility for courts to take a definitive stance.

Shifting outside from the United States, the Canadian Privacy Commission declared AI Clearview illegal in 2021, pointing out that it

---

[50] Trisha Mittal, 'A Summary of Concerns About Clearview AI's Facial Recognition Product', *Last Week in AI*, 11 March 2022 https://lastweekin.ai/p/clearview-ai-is-creating-facial-recognition accessed 31 July 2024.

[51] American Civil Liberties Union, '*ACLU v. Clearview AI*' https://www.aclu.org/cases/aclu-v-clearview-ai accessed 31 July 2024.

is 'unacceptable for millions of people who will never be implicated in any crime to find themselves continually in a police lineup'.[52] In the same year, the Australian Information and Privacy Commissioner held that AI Clearview handles 'personal information in a way that could have serious consequences for individuals whose information was collected'.[53] Due to these decisions, the use of Clearview should have stopped, yet there are reports that it is still being used at least in Australia,[54] while the contract with the Canadian authority has been terminated.

Other data protection authorities did not issue a general ban, but rather called on AI Clearview to adjust its standards to make it more compliant with data protection law. This happened, e.g., in Austria in 2023, with the Datenschutzbehörde (i.e., the federal data protection authority) highlighting that AI Clearview should at least have a clear deletion policy for the data of Austrian people.[55] And a similar decision had been taken a year before, in 2022, by the Italian data protection authority, claiming that AI Clearview had to erase the biometric data of thousands of Italians, collected through the web, and establish a clearer data collection policy for the future.[56]

---

[52] Office of the Privacy Commissioner of Canada, 'Clearview AI's Unlawful Practices Represented Mass Surveillance of Canadians, Commissioners Say', 3 February 2021 https://www.priv.gc.ca/en/opc-news/news-and-announcements/2021/nr-c_210203/ accessed 31 July 2024.

[53] Office of the Australian Information Commissioner, Clearview AI Breached Australians' Privacy, 3 November 2021 https://www.oaic.gov.au/newsroom/clearview-ai-breached-australians-privacy accessed 31 July 2024. The decision was taken after a joint investigation with the UK's Information Commissioner's Office.

[54] Cam Wilson, 'World's Most Controversial Company Clearview AI Still Being Used to Solve Australian Police Cases', Crikey, 25 January 2024 https://www.crikey.com.au/2024/01/25/clearview-ai-australian-police-operation-renewed-hope/ accessed 31 July 2024.

[55] Datenschutzbehörde https://noyb.eu/sites/default/files/2023-05/Clearview%20Decision%20Redacted.pdf accessed 31 July 2024.

[56] Garante per la Protezione dei Dati Personali (Italy), 'Riconoscimento facciale: il Garante privacy sanziona Clearview per 20 milioni di euro. Vietato l'uso dei dati biometrici e il monitoraggio degli italiani', 9 March 2022 https://www.garanteprivacy.it/home/docweb/-/docweb-display/docweb/9751323 accessed 31 July 2024.

This short overview is one of the many demonstrations that the use of biometric data is an issue with a transnational dimension: if US agencies rely on Clearview, this will affect, beyond US citizens, many more persons, e.g., in Italy, who have their content posted on the internet; if a company located in Europe buys the same service for commercial purposes, this will affect Canada; and so on. In other words, biometric technologies, especially when managed by private entities, entail a huge 'butterfly effect'. In the conclusions of this book, we will get back to the issue of transnationality brought by the interplay between technology and national security measures.

Going ahead with our analysis, we have examined until now a couple of central differences among facial recognition systems widely used by US federal law enforcement agencies (and also, as said, by other public and private bodies around the world); however, these software applications also show common points that need to be remarked upon because they are crucial from a legal perspective.

The first aspect that they all have in common is that they are used in the practice of law enforcement agencies, even if none of them is backed by a law specifically authorising their use. Such a lack of a legislative basis represents a common trait also in comparison with the addressed European scenario. To remedy (albeit not appropriately) this fault, some agencies passed internal guidelines and made privacy assessments on how to use facial recognition software in compliance with, e.g., privacy and data protection standards.[57] Yet, it is quite evident that guidelines and internal assessments are not 'law' in its proper sense, being mere internal acts of the agency that do not apply *erga omnes* and, most of all, are not legally binding outside of the agency itself. Rather, a legal basis – meant as an act of Congress, in the case of the US – would bind not only the agency but also the private entities that develop the application to follow certain standards. And, what is more, the constitutionality of a law can be challenged before courts, and this is a further, important, guarantee.

---

[57] See, e.g., Privacy Impact Assessment for the Facial Analysis, Comparison, and Evaluation (FACE) Services Unit https://www.fbi.gov/how-we-can-help-you/more-fbi-services-and-information/freedom-of-information-privacy-act/department-of-justice-fbi-privacy-impact-assessments/facial-analysis-comparison-and-evaluation-face-services-unit accessed 31 July 2024.

The second common feature is that all these systems, to be used by federal agencies' employees, would require them to be thoroughly trained in order to be fully aware of how these applications work, what their risks are, which mistakes they can make and how to fix them, and so on. Nevertheless, again, there is no legal requirement – in terms of federal law or regulation – that federal employees must receive training before starting to use these systems and relying on them in their job. Some internal rules of the agencies impose such training[58] without, again, it being a legal requirement. Although this might seem more an 'administrative' duty than a feature with legal consequences from the legal viewpoint, this is not the case. As a matter of fact, the less federal employees are well informed and trained on how to use these tools, the more likely it will be that they apply this technology in a way that may infringe on rights and freedoms.

Until this moment, we have addressed the US federal level and compared it with other experiences. Turning to the state level, it is not the aim of this analysis to examine each and every one of the 50 federated states of the US Federation; nonetheless, a comprehensive overview of how state police resort to facial recognition technology can be useful and fits much better the purpose of the present work. Quite surprisingly, the legislation of some states is far more restrictive than the federal scenario. In fact, there are some US states where the use of facial recognition by the police is prohibited, with very few exceptions. This is the case of Vermont,[59] where the use of facial recognition by the state police is absolutely prohibited, with the only exception of crimes of child sexual exploitation. Other states pose fewer limitations. For instance, according to Oregon's legislation,[60] facial recognition can be used by state police as long as the police do not use body cameras at the same time. Then, there are states where a wider use of facial recognition is allowed. Among others, in Virginia[61] facial recognition can be used by the police for a list of specific crimes, including acts of terrorism.

At the same time, it must be noted that several municipalities in the United States are passing their own regulations on facial recognition,[62]

[58] In particular, these agencies are the HSI, the USMS, and the USSS.
[59] 8 2020 Vermont Acts and Resolves 799 s 14.
[60] 2019 Oregon Revised Statutes s 133.741.
[61] 2020 Vermont Acts and Resolves 799.
[62] Mailyn Fidler and Justin (Gus) Hurwitz, *op. cit.*, 214.

generally allowing it but with limits (e.g., by restricting the list of crimes for which it can be used).

Therefore, the general picture shows that regulation is more stringent at the state (and local) level than at the federal level, which applies a laissez-faire approach, in line with the traditional stance of the United States vis-à-vis privacy issues. This proactivity of state and local levels, compared with the Federation, could be explained in different ways, none of which appears convincing. First, state and local regulations can be passed more quickly than federal ones, due to the fact that their debate does not involve the United States as a whole. This is, of course, true for legislation on any topic, yet such a sensitive one would need as accurate a consideration as possible. Second, state and local rules are going to have an effect on a more limited number of people than federal legislation, and this may contribute to a lower weighting in the competent bodies. However, affecting a (relatively) small number of people does not mean that potential implications on their rights and freedom deserve less consideration. Third, in the same way as they are relatively quick to be passed, they are also quick to be amended. In other words, the state and local levels have more flexibility than the federal level in passing regulation. However, given the wide effects that the use of biometrics in law enforcement has, the federal level would be, in theory, better placed to legislate on these topics, so federal regulation of the matter would be highly desirable, even considering the fact that it touches upon national (and not only local) security, an undoubtedly federal competence. Moreover, it appears that, given the need to interact with private entities and, to some extent, negotiate with them, such cooperation and negotiation would be better achieved by federal authorities than by state or local ones.

Against this background, the United States does not even have, so far, a federal law on general privacy issues, so the path towards the regulation of facial recognition is likely to be a very 'bumpy ride'.

6. 'Chasing' the terrorist threat: technologies for 'personalised' surveillance

Within the taxonomy we have introduced to classify counter-terrorism measures based on technology, another relevant way to use advanced tools in measures against terrorism is to chase those people who have already been identified as representing a threat. 'Chase' here means that technology is used either to trace the activity of those suspected people – and take all the necessary steps to apprehend and prosecute them – or to monitor the actions of already convicted people.

From a general legal viewpoint, it appears that these measures, if compared to bulk surveillance, are less impactful on principles such as the presumption of innocence. This is because 'chasing' tools only target those people who have already been identified as a threat; hence, from a legal perspective, they can be qualified as targeted or individual surveillance. Although this statement is undoubtedly true, a couple of observations tone it down. First, in order to ascertain who, among the general social community, poses a threat, mass surveillance techniques are usually applied *ex ante*, i.e., before this kind of 'personalised' surveillance. This means that, to target *one* person, *all* people are previously subjected to surveillance (addressed in the chaptersabove). Second, measures aimed at tracing one person who is, e.g., a suspected terrorist often inevitably entail interferences with the privacy of all other people who interact with him/her and might not be suspected of any crime (so-called collateral intrusion).

Coming to the substance of these measures, 'chasing' counter-terrorism activities are mostly represented by several forms of interceptions. The object of interceptions can be communications between people through different means (email, telephone, chat, etc.) as well as other confidential information, e.g., financial operations made through bank accounts. When the object of the interception is communications, this implies that investigating authorities grab the *content* of communications, and not just the information around them (metadata). Similarly, when the interception regards other data – we have just given the example of bank operations – the content of these activities is recorded (e.g., how much money is transferred, to whom, etc.). In this way, these interception techniques differ from all those measures – which we have examined above – based on the collection of metadata, as the latter does not include any access to communication content.

Interceptions have been regulated by domestic criminal legislation for a long time, and they are used to prosecute a high number of serious crimes of a different nature, not just in the field of counter-terrorism.[1] As a general trend, the more serious a crime is considered, the more intrusive the interception measures will be, according to the application of the principle of proportionality.

However, although interceptions undoubtedly play a major role in 'chasing' activities, there is also a second set of measures that deserve consideration in this part. Reference is made to all those monitoring tools – like, e.g., traditional electronic bracelets and more updated tools we will survey – that are resorted to when suspected (or even already convicted) people are subjected to restrictions of their personal freedom.

The following sections address both categories of measures, interceptions and monitoring tools, always paying specific attention to the most advanced technology methods, often grounded in artificial intelligence.

1. THE INTERCEPTION OF COMMUNICATIONS AS A COUNTER-TERRORISM TOOL

Interceptions can be carried out in several ways, spanning from the most 'analogical' ones – let us think, among others, of espionage, implying the physical presence of a spy to monitor the activities and conversations of suspected individuals – to the use of the most cutting-edge technology tools – let us think, among others, of wiretaps, telephone bugging, laser technologies, and spyware (also called Trojan horses for the reasons we will address *infra*).

[1] From the perspective of its impact on privacy, see Normann Witzleb, David Lindsay, Moira Paterson and Sharon Rodrick (eds), *Emerging Challenges in Privacy Law. Comparative Perspective* (CUP 2014).

Given the focus of this work, we now take into consideration the latter set of methods and, before digging into its legal regulation, we first give an overview of how the latest technologies can be used to intercept single persons, or groups of persons, suspected of terrorist activities.

1.1 Technical Functioning of Advanced Interception Techniques

When we glance at the technology methods that make interceptions possible,[2] we can identify four main groups of technology tools that can be resorted to, and we can list and explain them, going from the most ancient to the most recent.

A first category of techniques gathers those tools relying on wiretaps. Wiretaps are physical objects that are placed within a certain distance of the person who is intercepted and are able to grab the content of a conversation. Wiretaps can be based either on radio waves or on the GSM/UMTS technology. While the former, i.e., radio waves, only allows short-distance interceptions, the latter, i.e., GSM/UMTS, works through cell phone towers, in a way very similar to a SIM card.[3] This means that GSM/UMTS technologies are able to intercept conversations taking place at a very long distance from where the spyware is placed. These technologies – both radio waves and GSM/UMTS tools – have existed for a very long time, so they can be considered among the most ancient ones, and do not imply any form of automation, unless interceptions are transcribed, a stage where intelligent algorithms can turn out to be very useful. Notwithstanding the fact that they are 'aging', they are still widely used around the world, often combined with other investigatory techniques, not always relying on technology.

[2] Organization for Security and Co-operation in Europe (OSCE), 'Human Rights in Counter-Terrorism Investigations. A Practical Manual for Law Enforcement Officers' (2013) https://www.osce.org/files/f/documents/5/f/108930.pdf accessed 31 July 2024.

[3] On the evolution of interception methods, from the most ancient ones onwards, see Kerstin Goos, Michael Friedewald, C. William R. Webster and Charles Leleux, 'The Co-evolution of Surveillance Technologies and Surveillance Practices' in David Wright and Reinhard Kreissl (eds), *Surveillance in Europe* (Routledge 2014) 52.

A second type of technology, still widespread in law enforcement activities despite being quite outdated as well, is telephone bugging, i.e. traditional telephone interceptions.[4] This technique is based on the cooperation between investigating authorities and telephone communication providers, with the former asking the latter – who are bound to comply – to duplicate telephone lines. More clearly, if telephone line A connects individual X (who is, e.g., a suspected terrorist) to individual Y (his/her interlocutor), the telephone company is ordered to create a parallel telephone line (which we can call line B) connecting the investigating authorities to the conversation between X and Y. In this way, the authorities can hear real-time conversations, record them, and have them transcribed, if needed. As with traditional wiretapping, telephone bugging does not normally rely on automated algorithms, since it limits itself to exploiting telephone connections, which do not work on the basis of artificial intelligence. Importantly, telephone bugging can be used only when the communication takes place on traditional telephone lines; hence, it does not apply to calls through WhatsApp and other services that allow phone calls by relying on internet connection and encryption. This is one of the main reasons why new tools needed to be developed, 'evolving into' spyware (see *infra*). In fact, nowadays people's communication relies more and more on encrypted services – such as WhatsApp – so applying traditional interception techniques would not yield any result.

A third set of technologies that make interceptions of conversations possible is grounded in laser technologies.[5] These are microphones, available to many law enforcement authorities around the world, containing a laser wave that is directed towards a specific place or building and is able to intercept the vibrations coming from sounds emitted therein. Specific software then transforms these vibrations into audio files, which can, in turn be transcribed. These technologies are more advanced than the previous two since they rely on a laser beam, a type of technology developed more recently than wiretaps and telephone lines.

---

[4] For a legal and sociological overview of how wiretapping models were framed in Europe and in the United States, see Lora A. Esau, 'The Correlation between Wiretapping and Terrorism: A Comparative Analysis of American and European Societal Views on Government Surveillance' (2016) 23 ILSA J Intl Comp L 55.

[5] João G.M. Gonçalves, Vítor Sequeira and Julian Whichello, 'Laser Technologies for On-Site Surveillance', IAEA-SM-367/7/06.

The fourth method is the use of spyware, and this is the most interesting method from our perspective, as well as one of the most discussed tools in the fight against serious crime, including terrorism.[6] Spyware is a software that can be introduced in a device (computer, smartphone, tablet, etc.) without the consent of its owner and, most of all, without him/her realising that an external software was put in the device. For this reason, they are sometimes referred to as 'Trojan horses'. Interestingly, the spyware is a sort of 'well-intentioned' version of the malware that we analysed in Part I as one among the techniques that terrorists use to carry out their cyber-attacks; as a matter of fact, the spyware is nothing but a malware, yet it is used for law enforcement purposes to repress crime, so it acts 'on the good side'.

This double-faced nature of technology is a clear demonstration of the ambiguity we have mentioned several times throughout this volume.

Coming back to the functioning of the spyware, once introduced on a device, this tool is able to trace the activities carried out by the target device and send the data to whoever installed the spyware. Sometimes, the spyware can even work by screenshotting the activities of the target, thus providing an exact record of what a user did. As a result, the use of spyware is able to overcome the difficulties faced by previous technologies in accessing, e.g., WhatsApp messages and other instant messaging apps. Actually, end-to-end encryption is undermined by the fact that the spyware is able to take screenshots. Moreover, and importantly, spyware may allow investigating authorities to monitor activities on the dark web,[7] something that would otherwise prove very challenging, as we explained earlier in this work. This has been labelled as full-fledged 'hacking' activity by law enforcement or intelligence bodies.[8] In the use

---

[6] Amnesty International, 'What is Spyware and What Can You Do to Stay Protected?' 14 December 2023 https://www.amnesty.org/en/latest/campaigns/2023/12/what-is-spyware-and-what-you-can-do-to-stay-protected/ accessed 31 July 2024. For a critical reading of spyware technologies, Siena Anstis, Jakub Dalek and Ronald J. Deibert, 'The Ethical and Legal Dilemmas of Digital Accountability Research and the Utility of International Norm-Setting' (2024) 118 AJIL 40.

[7] Eldar Haber, 'The Law of the Trojan Horse' (2024) 57 UC Davis LR 1667.

[8] Quentin Liger and Mirja Gutheil, 'The Use of Pegasus and Equivalent Surveillance Spyware. The Existing Legal Framework in EU Member States for the Acquisition and Use of Pegasus and Equivalent Surveillance

of spyware, artificial intelligence may come into play, insofar as intelligent algorithms could enhance the activity of the installed software, for instance by combining the collected information to measure the likelihood that a suspected person actually committed a crime, again relying on artificial intelligence prevention potential. So far, and based on available data, no system of this kind, merging spyware technology – which is already very advanced – and artificial intelligence, has been openly deployed by law enforcement and intelligence bodies around the world. Nevertheless, we need to bear in mind that the use of these systems is often carried out without transparency, so it cannot be excluded that these strategies are resorted to but not disclosed to the general public.

This scenario shows that the use of spyware is undoubtedly the most advanced form of interception that law enforcement and intelligence authorities have at their disposal so far. Therefore, the next section will focus specifically on it, by examining the practice and – where existent – the legal regulation of these tools in the main advanced democracies, always from a comparative viewpoint.

1.2 Legal Regulation and Practice in the Use of Spyware

The nature of spyware urged a number of State authorities to use it, especially in the investigation of the most serious crimes. Terrorism-related crimes seem to be the perfect candidate in this regard. These tools are highly effective since they 'photograph' anything happening on a device. Notwithstanding their effectiveness, the invasion of privacy and, most of all, the risks of abuses connected to their use make them a potential danger for rule-of-law-based systems.

Going into the details of spyware, one of the most well-known among these tools is Pegasus, developed by an Israeli company.[9] In addition to Pegasus, there are hundreds of equivalent applications designed by other

Spyware', European Parliament, Study for the PEGA Committee, 5 December 2022 https://www.europarl.europa.eu/thinktank/en/document/IPOL_STU(2022)740151 accessed 31 July 2024.

[9] Giovanni Sartor and Andrea Loreggia, 'The Impact of Pegasus on Fundamental Rights and Democratic Processes', European Parliament (EP), Research Study published for the PEGA Committee, 5 December 2022 https://www.europarl.europa.eu/RegData/etudes/STUD/2022/740514/IPOL_STU(2022)740514_EN.pdf accessed 9 February 2025.

companies, less known but working in a similar way. The reason why Pegasus is the most well-known spyware is that it sparked a scandal in 2021, when some investigative journalists and civil society organisations started disclosing that many governments around the world used Pegasus for further – and possibly unlawful – purposes than investigations against crime.[10] Pegasus was also claimed to be used for political aims against journalists, politicians, activists, and other public personalities, including even diplomats. Thus, Pegasus was allegedly employed as a tool enhancing the repression of political dissent, rather than as a technique to investigate crimes. After the scandal, the European Parliament (EP) appointed an inquiry commission to investigate the use of Pegasus by governments of both Member States and some third countries as well. The commission reported[11] to the EP in March 2023. The EP then adopted a set of resolutions, whose content will be addressed later in this section, on how to stem the abuse of spyware like Pegasus.

Before focussing on how potential abuses can be prevented or minimised, it is worth providing a comparative overview of the use of Pegasus and similar technologies. Our analysis concentrates on the *lawful* uses of these tools by public authorities, i.e., in circumstances like the investigation aimed at the apprehension of culprits and the prosecution of crimes. Since this is a criminal law topic, there is no detailed supranational framework – criminal law being a field still very much left to State sovereignty – regulating it, so it is necessary to dig into the criminal and procedural legislation, as well as investigation practices, of single States. To do this, as a first step, we look at the EU Member States by selecting some of them where available data show higher reliance on spyware; secondly, we open our perspective to the United Kingdom; we then consider the United States; and lastly, we take into account some other countries that have been demonstrated to rely heavily on these

---

[10] See European Parliament, Plenary, Investigation of the Use of Pegasus and Equivalent Surveillance Spyware, PE 747.923 –June 2023 https://www.europarl.europa.eu/RegData/etudes/ATAG/2023/747923/EPRS_ATA(2023)747923_IT.pdf accessed 31 July 2024.

[11] European Parliament, Report of the investigation of alleged contraventions and maladministration in the application of Union law in relation to the use of Pegasus and equivalent surveillance spyware, 25 May 2023, (2022/2077(INI)) https://www.europarl.europa.eu/doceo/document/A-9-2023-0189_IT.html accessed 31 July 2024.

tools, namely Australia and New Zealand. In order to examine these four different scenarios, we apply a common scheme that allows us to carry out horizontal, and not merely vertical, comparison.

According to this scheme, we first look at which bodies can ask for authorisation to use spyware in criminal investigations; second, we take into account which bodies, in each country, can authorise the use of spyware; and third, we consider which crimes allow the use of these technologies.

Starting from Member States of the European Union, the rules for resorting to spyware are contained in codes of criminal procedures or in subsequent laws which amend them to update their contents to technological innovations (e.g. in Italy, Legislative Decree no. 216/2017). In most EU countries, the request to use spyware may come from public prosecutors within criminal investigations (e.g. in Italy, the Netherlands, and Spain), although in some cases (France and Germany are examples) it may come even from police officials or intelligence services, without the need to hear a jurisdictional authority beforehand. For instance, in Italy, this authorisation (which is referred to as a 'warrant' in Anglo-Saxon countries) is the task of the giudice per le indagini preliminari, i.e., a judge who oversees the criminal proceeding only at the investigation stage and has no role in deciding on the guilt or innocence of the accused person. Yet, when, as in France or Germany, the authorising body depends on the executive, potential infringement of due process may arise, since police and intelligence officials do not share the same guarantees of independence as judges.

Looking at the objective scope of spyware regulation, criminal procedure codes of EU Member States use some common criteria to identify the crimes whose investigation allows reliance on spyware. One criterion is the conduct of the crime: terrorism, paedo-pornography, drug crimes, and organised crime, in general, are often considered among the most serious ones[12] and, consequently, investigating authorities are often legitimised to use spyware when they carry out inquiries on them (e.g., this happens in the Italian legal system). This is because these crimes are commonly considered among the most serious ones, so proceeding against them can allow reliance on such intrusive technologies. Another criterion, frequently as an alternative to the first one, is based on the sanction required for the crime: in some countries, police and intelligence bodies

---

[12] E.g., in Italy and Germany.

cannot use spyware unless they are proceeding for a crime requiring a minimum period of imprisonment (e.g., four years in the Netherlands). Indeed, this criterion still relies on the seriousness of the crime, yet from another perspective, i.e., the amount of the sanction rather than the type of conduct. Other countries – Germany is an example – only rely on quite a vague criterion of proportionality. Specifically, based on this criterion, the legislation merely requires that there is proportionality between the seriousness of the crime and the invasiveness of the investigative method and that no less intrusive means would be as effective as the installation of a spyware system. This is a more discretionary criterion, which may prove useful in allowing flexibility to authorities but implies the risk of possible instrumentalisation if used incorrectly.

Applying the same scheme of analysis to the United Kingdom – whose comparison with EU countries is always useful and methodologically sound, due to their tight relationships even after Brexit – we can see that the Investigatory Powers Act 2016[13] allows UK law enforcement agencies and intelligence services to request the use of spyware in their investigation. The request is assessed and authorised by the Secretary of State for the Home Department if he/she deems that prerequisites exist. Notably, the State Secretary is a member of the Cabinet and not a judicial authority, so UK law seems more disrespectful vis-à-vis the separation of powers than the EU Member States addressed above. Like in Germany, in the UK it is enough that a vaguely expressed principle of proportionality is respected to decide whether or not to authorise spyware. More clearly, according to the Investigatory Powers Act, the State Secretary can authorise these tools if he/she considers it 'proportionate to what is sought to be achieved'.[14] As a whole, the UK rules appear to leave much discretion to (non-judicial) authorities and, consequently, contain several warnings that it may be prone to abuse.

Shifting to the United States, the use of spyware is not specifically regulated by any federal law, so US federal law enforcement and intelligence agencies admitted to a wide use of these technology resources in their investigations, also backed by the traditional concept of privacy as a recessive interest when weighed against other interests, such as national security. The only indirect reference to spyware can be found in a 2016 amendment to the Federal Rules of Criminal Procedure (FRCP).

---

[13] Investigatory Powers Act 2016, c. 25.

[14] Investigatory Powers Act 2016, sec. 19(1)(b).

According to Rule 41 FRCP, law enforcement and intelligence agencies can gain access to 'remote data' when they request and obtain a warrant from a judge; the warrant can even exceed the territorial jurisdiction of the United States, meaning that interception can apply to US citizens abroad or even to non-US citizens. This is a clear example of the extraterritorial application of a legal provision, aimed at enhancing the security of a certain State community. The need to request a warrant implies that, at least according to the rationale of Rule 41 FRCP, the use of spyware falls within the definition of a 'search' under the Fourth Amendment to the US Constitution. The Fourth Amendment requires that searches, to be authorised under a warrant, have to be 'reasonable'. Hence, in the United States there is no list of crimes for which spyware can be used, being only limited by the reasonableness requirement under the Fourth Amendment – and its related case law[15] – which needs to be respected. In this regard, the United States present an analogy to those European countries where a proportionality assessment is required, as in Germany.

Nonetheless, as some scholars remarked,[16] there might be interpretations according to which spyware escapes from the application of the Fourth Amendment (and, thus, of the reasonableness requirement as well as of the need for a warrant) due to the third-party doctrine. Under this well-known doctrine,[17] once a user allows a third party – e.g., a communication provider – to access information, the user loses any privacy expectation over that data. As a rebuttal, it could be pointed out that many digital services (e.g., WhatsApp, Telegram, etc.) that spyware is able to access indeed apply end-to-end encryption, so the user actually *did not* authorise the provider's company to access their communication. As in other fields that we have examined throughout this work, the US scenario appears to be among the most 'uncertain' in terms of regulation of technology, and this overview on spyware confirms this statement.

To complete the overview of North America, the Canadian approach to spyware is noteworthy, too. Like in the United States, the Canadian police admitted to wide use of spyware, deemed necessary to overcome

[15] See Jennifer Stisa Granick, *American Spies: Modern Surveillance, Why You Should Care, and What to Do About It* (CUP 2017) 217.

[16] Eldar Haber, *op. cit.*

[17] *Katz v. United States*, 389 US 347 (1967); *United States v. Miller*, 425 US 435 (1976); *Smith v. Maryland*, 442 US 735 (1979).

encryption, which makes surveillance increasingly difficult.[18] Canada has no legal framework to regulate spyware, and commentators have shown serious concerns about the fact that this technology is being used only in practice.[19] Thus, the Canadian scenario is very much like the US one, with a sort of 'migration' of the stance taken by public authorities regarding the use of this intrusive surveillance tool. Usually, Canadian privacy standards are higher than those in the United States, and the fact that, in this case, they are harmonising with the US ones can be seen as symptomatic of a certain lowering of guarantees worldwide, at least when national security is at stake.

Leaving behind the North American panorama, a wide resort to spyware technology in the field of criminal investigation, and more specifically of counter-terrorism, is made in Australia and New Zealand, two countries that, although not geographically part of the 'Western world', can easily be compared to main Western advanced democracies due to historical, cultural, and legal reasons. As we will immediately see, in these countries, legislation on spyware is quite harsh, yet with the advantage that, at least, this tool is regulated, unlike with the United States and Canada.

Starting from Australia, according to the Surveillance Legislation Amendment (Identify and Disrupt) Act 2021,[20] officers of the Australian Federal Police and of the Australian Criminal Intelligence Commission can apply for a warrant to a judge to use disruptive technologies (i.e., those technologies aimed at accessing and copying data contained in a device). In deciding whether or not to allow the use of these technologies – which, given the above definition, include spyware – the judge must weigh several elements. The first feature is the seriousness of the conduct; second, whether using these technologies is the only possible

[18] Maura Forrest, 'Canada's National Police Force Admits Use of Spyware to Hack Phones', *Politico*, 29 June 2022 https://www.politico.com/news/2022/06/29/canada-national-police-spyware-phones-00043092 accessed 31 July 2024.

[19] Greg McMullen, 'Pulling Back the Curtain on Canada's Mass Surveillance Programs – Part One: A Decade of Secret Spy Hearings', *British Columbia Civil Liberties Association*, 14 December 2022 https://bccla.org/2022/12/pulling-back-the-curtain-on-canadas-mass-surveillance-programs-part-one-a-decade-of-secret-spy-hearings/ accessed 31 July 2024.

[20] Surveillance Legislation Amendment (Identify and Disrupt) Act 2021.

means to conduct the investigation, or alternative and less intrusive means would exist; third, what would be the impact on third parties, including on individuals' privacy; and fourth, whether it would impact journalists conducting investigations in the public interest. Thus, in Australia, the authorisation is given by an independent body – a judge – yet the assessment he/she has to perform is quite discretionary, since the criteria are wide.

Focussing on a country that is very close to Australia, not only geographically but also culturally, in New Zealand there was a significant crackdown in spyware legislation after the 2019 Christchurch attack and the 2021 Auckland supermarket stabbing. Based on the Counter-Terrorism Legislation Act 2021,[21] the police and the security services can carry out warrantless surveillance against people suspected of having committed terrorist acts, without any need for authorisation, which is particularly concerning. This activity may include surveillance performed through advanced technology tools, like spyware. Thus, although New Zealand – like Australia – at least regulates spyware, its legislation appears to be among the most worrying, insofar as the need for a warrant is substantively bypassed, so it could be easily classified as the most 'draconian' among the ones analysed until this moment.

From a general angle, it can be seen that practically all advanced democracies use spyware in their investigative practices, albeit they do not always regulate it in a clear and detailed way and, most of all, with a view to safeguarding human rights such as privacy and the protection of users' data. Moreover, States do not always disclose their resort to spyware, thereby undermining even the principle of transparency and the trust relationship that should link citizens and public bodies in a democratic country. To this, one should add that – as hinted at the beginning of our analysis of spyware – the malicious use of this technology easily lies behind, making it a sort of 'slippery slope.'

At this point, it is worth examining more in depth how spyware can be abused, and what have been, until now, the main guidelines that have been drawn in order to avoid the mischievous resort to these tools.

Regarding the risk of abuse, it should be borne in mind that spyware, like Pegasus and other related tools, are developed by private companies, which can sell them to governments and – what is most troubling – to other private companies and to governments of non-democratic

[21] Counter-Terrorism Legislation Act 2021.

countries. This means that this technology can be used for purely commercial purposes as well as for full-fledged and unlawful espionage performed for political aims. For instance, the European Parliament,[22] in its recommendation issued in June 2023 after examining the report of the inquiry commission on the abuses of Pegasus, claimed that the latter was used by the governments of Morocco and Rwanda – among others – to target European leaders (e.g. the Prime Ministers of Belgium and France and the former Prime Minister of Italy).

After the Pegasus scandal, recommendations and suggestions came from both supranational institutions (such as the European Parliament and even the Parliamentary Assembly of the Council of Europe[23]) as well as from groups of States,[24] which joined forces to guarantee that the use of spyware, deemed essential to guarantee security, does not amount to abuses and human rights violations. The core of these recommendations can be synthetically analysed in the remainder, in order to assess whether they could be effective and in which ways they could be implemented.

One of the most common suggestions found in these documents is that spyware should be regulated by a supranational framework (e.g. the EU in the European area, as suggested by the EP's recommendation), which could be able to steer the approach of criminal legislation enacted by individual countries. In our view, this would indeed be an essential step to guarantee supranational oversight and, in some cases, a clearer legal basis for the use of spyware. Nevertheless, attention should be paid not to provide an excessively vague supranational framework, leaving too much discretion to State bodies, as often happens in the field of security (and, most of all, of security measures based on technology). Rather, a supranational piece of legislation should be clear and precise enough,

---

[22] European Parliament, Investigation of the Use of Pegasus and Equivalent Surveillance Spyware (Recommendation), P9_TA(2023)0244 https://www.europarl.europa.eu/doceo/document/TA-9-2023-0244_EN.html accessed 31 July 2024.

[23] Council of Europe, Parliamentary Assembly, 'Pegasus and Similar Spyware and Secret State Surveillance', Doc. 15825, 20 September 2023 https://pace.coe.int/en/files/33018 accessed 31 July 2024.

[24] E.g., in March 2023, Australia, Canada, Costa Rica, Denmark, France, New Zealand, Norway, Sweden, Switzerland, the United Kingdom, and the United States made a joint statement declaring their will to engage in cooperation to prevent abuses of spyware not only in their domestic legal systems, but also internationally.

and be framed in a way to include the voice of private companies as well, given their non-renounceable role.

Another recommendation that these documents provide is that the people who are targeted by these disruptive technologies would need to be informed. This approach is a very right-protective one, perfectly compliant with the transparency principle and the maintaining of a fair relationship of trust between States and their citizens. Nonetheless, it could be strongly criticised by law enforcement and intelligence bodies, insofar as informing the person who is targeted by the spyware could seriously frustrate the output of their investigative activities. Thus, a balance should be found, e.g. by providing clarity, in domestic legislation, about which crimes can be investigated through 'Trojans', without leaving the choice to excessively vague application of the proportionality principle by single investigating and jurisdictional authorities. In this way, certainty of law, as a basic principle of the rule of law, would be enhanced as well.

A further suggestion coming from these guidelines is that only countries where previous abuses of Pegasus (and similar technologies) have been thoroughly investigated should be allowed to use these tools in the future. Although this is a 'right-minded' recommendation, it may seem unlikely that all the countries in which Pegasus abuses have been alleged will perform independent investigations. This could be compensated by the setup of a supranational committee tasked with investigating and provided with sharper powers than, for example, the one established by the EU, which could only make 'soft law' recommendations. Albeit they would not be binding, they could exercise a certain amount of moral suasion.

As anticipated at the beginning of this section, interceptions, in particular through spyware, are not the only 'chasing' tool that law enforcement authorities have at their disposal. The next section will thus focus on monitoring technologies, usually applied to suspects or even to those who have already been convicted.

2. MONITORING TECHNOLOGIES AS COUNTER-TERRORISM TOOLS

The use of monitoring technologies to track suspects of crimes has been very common since the first developments of the Global Positioning System (GPS) technology. These tools are used to track the positions of suspected terrorists or, in some cases, of people subjected to pre-trial detention or even convicted and placed under house arrest. Thus, tools like electronic bracelets cannot be defined as advanced or new technologies, since they have existed for a long time. Nonetheless, very recently, studies are being carried out on how to merge 'old' monitoring technologies with artificial intelligence, possibly even putting an end to detention as we know it and bringing incarceration to new forms. These systems are still at the trial or experimental stage, and for this reason, the structure of this section will be partially different from the previous ones. We will still provide a framework of how these systems – applying algorithms to the geographical positioning of convicted or suspected individuals – may technically work if deployed. Although we cannot analyse how they are legally regulated since, as stated, most of them are still being studied and are under discussion, we can engage in an analysis of the legal implications and issues that their use would entail.

2.1 Technical Functioning of Monitoring Technologies (Merged with Artificial Intelligence)

Starting from 2017, some studies have been brought forward by a team of Australian scholars,[25] aiming to monitor systems – similar to traditional GPS-based electronic bracelets – that would incorporate a sophisticated sensor capable of detecting any intention to commit a new crime or a violation of the applicable legal framework. This would be possible thanks to a combination of GPS technology and intelligent algorithms. More specifically, GPS would be needed – as in traditional monitoring tools – to make sure that individuals placed under detention do not move outside of the place where they are required to stay. Additionally – and here artificial intelligence comes into play – an algorithm would be trained to recognise dangerous actions, behaviour, or even conversations. Thirdly, the study to which we referred even proposes that the algorithm, once it recognises unlawful behavioural schemes, sends a message to a system capable of immobilising the person remotely, like a taser or a stun gun activated by a computer, without causing serious injury to him/her. Once the person is immobilised, law enforcement bodies would be called, still thanks to an alarm sent by the device itself. Such a system has been

[25] Mirko Bagaric, Dan Hunter and Gabrielle Wolf, 'Technological Incarceration and the End of the Prison Crisis' (2018) 108 J of Crim L and Criminology 73.

proposed as a strategy aimed, among other things, to deflate prison overcrowding, a problem that affects several advanced democracies, and create a system of 'smart prisons' or 'technological incarceration'. So far, there is no evidence that such a system – or a similar one – has already been applied in all its steps in any region of the world, but some tests incorporating one or another of these elements have been run.[26] For instance, some prisons located in the United States are experimenting with a device called 'Talitrix Inside the Walls', wearable by prisoners and able to monitor their location, their interactions, their heart rate, and calculate the risk that they engage in the commission of offences or attempt to flee. Further studies are being carried out to apply the analysis of facial expressions to detect emotions and intentions. However, this is something that, at least in the EU environment, would be promptly blocked, insofar as the new AI regulation (AI Act) prohibits the use of emotion analysis as a predictive police technique.[27]

2.2 Legal Issues Arising from the (Prospective) Resort to 'Technological Incarceration'

At first glance, resorting to technological incarceration as explained above might seem a very valuable method to tackle the problem of prison overcrowding as well as to use technology in a functional and effective way to assist law enforcement activities. However, awareness should be raised about several legal issues that, although not being, in our view, absolutely preclusive to the use of these techniques, should at least be a warning against possible abuses of these systems.

Some challenging aspects that we point out regard technological incarceration in general, without any specific reference to the type of offender to whom it is applied; others, instead, refer to the possibility of applying these tools to terrorist offenders.

Starting from the general legal issues of technological detention, a first, quite evident possible problem has to do with the right to privacy, and, well before this, with the right to personal freedom. The combination of GPS technology and artificial intelligence means that the person

---

[26] Federica Fedorczyk, 'It Is Time to Start Thinking about Smart Prisons', *LimaBlog*, March 2024 https://limablog.org/it-is-time-to-start-thinking-about-smart-prisons/ accessed 31 July 2024.

[27] Regulation (EU) 2024/1689, art. 5.1(f).

is constantly monitored, and his/her behavior assessed at any moment of the day. Such an approach appears to potentially violate the proportionality principle,[28] and even human dignity is under stress, whose respect should instead be a *conditio sine qua non* for compliance with the rule of law, independent of the seriousness of the committed crime and the advancement of technology used.

Furthermore, if the system described above was applied in its entirety, i.e., including the order of remote immobilisation, the consequence on the prisoner's right to physical integrity cannot be excluded. On this point, although it is true that the devices mentioned in the study (a taser or a stun gun) are unlikely to cause serious harm, they may still produce some harm on the body of a person, not to mention the psychological effects of such a system, impacting a person's right to mental health. Consequently, their use would amount to corporal punishment that, in a democratic environment compliant with the rule of law principles, needs to be avoided. Moreover, such harm would be inflicted by a machine – a remote computer assessing the behaviour of the inmate, which makes the whole thing much more problematic, since a computer cannot bear the same legal responsibility as a human would. Given this scenario, in our view, the third step of technological imprisonment should either be refined by introducing methods that make the offender desist from their criminal purpose without impacting their physical integrity, or not be resorted to.

Shifting to those issues that would be raised by the use of technological detention in the specific field of terrorist crimes, a significant problem appears to be its effectiveness. As explained, the main purpose of this technique would be to monitor the activity of a highly suspected or convicted person to prevent the reiteration of the same crime (or the commission of some other crime). In legal terms, we can say that it has a special-preventive aim, meaning trying to prevent a specific person from committing a crime or recommitting a crime he or she has already committed in the past. When terrorist or terrorist-related offences come into play, though, it seems very implausible that the planning of future terrorist attacks, or all the other offences linked to terrorism – e.g., conduct related to indoctrination, attempts to radicalise others, etc. – may take

[28] As elaborated by the case law of the European Court of Justice in its decisions about the balance between privacy and data protection, on the one hand, and national security, on the other hand. See *supra*.

place through explicit behavior. In other words, it is not necessary that the imprisoned person tries to flee or use weapons in order to attempt a terrorist offence. He/she could well resort to other tools, such as the internet and the media in general, to radicalise other people or even to self-indoctrinate. And the powerful and refined algorithm employed in this strategy would be able to monitor movements and actions, yet it would hardly be capable of recording such conduct, consisting, e.g., of surfing the internet. The only way to overcome this problem of effectiveness would be to use algorithms able to measure emotions and, consequently, predict intentions. Yet, as discussed above, resorting to this technology would be forbidden by most recent legislative acts.

Therefore, we argue that, given the present state of the art, the resort to technological incarceration would not be beneficial in terms of cost-benefit analysis – where costs consist of the infringement of rights and the risk of ineffectiveness, and benefits are the possibilities that this system works well in preventing and repressing crime – both in the prosecution of general crime *and* in the fight against terrorism. Rather, as has been argued by some scholars,[29] AI could be useful at another stage of the criminal law enforcement process, that is rehabilitation, as it is already being experimented in some Scandinavian countries.[30] In this regard, it has been demonstrated[31] that artificial intelligence can be very helpful in creating 'digital environments' that can be accessed by convicted people in order to be re-introduced to society, e.g., by progressively having them participate in workplaces, social interaction, etc. An experiment in this field has been conducted in Finland, where the University of Tampere is collaborating with the national Criminal Sanctions Agency to set up a programme using virtual reality to provide prison inmates with simulations of outdoor experiences. These methods could be particularly

---

29 Federica Fedorczyk, *op. cit.*; Anne Kaun and Fredrik Stiernstedt, 'Doing Time, the Smart Way? Temporalities of the Smart Prison' (2020) 22 New Media & Soc 1580; Eugenia Zivanai and Gilbert Mahlangu, 'Digital Prison Rehabilitation and Successful Re-entry into a Digital Society: A Systematic Literature Review on the New Reality on Prison Rehabilitation' (2022) 8 Cogent Social Sciences 2116809.

30 Y. Jewkes and B.C. Reisdorf, 'A Brave New World: The Problems and Opportunities Presented by New Media Technologies in Prisons' (2016) 16 Criminology & Criminal Justice 534.

31 Eugenia Zivanai and Gilbert Mahlangu, *op. cit.*

appropriate in contexts where the person who committed a terrorism-related offence needs to be de-radicalised since it would help reduce social isolation and make people feel involved in a community again. In other terms, artificial intelligence could be of great assistance in de-radicalisation programmes, a field that deserves further study also from a sociology and psychology viewpoint.

After having examined the use of advanced technologies to investigate and prosecute those who committed or are likely to have committed terrorist crimes, it is worth digging into the last, and probably most slippery, use of technology for counter-terrorism purposes, that is the shaping of public opinion. The next chapter is dedicated to this peculiar technique.

7. Technology and counter-terrorism: shaping public opinion

The use of media to shape public opinion is certainly not a novelty of the so-called digital age. Since their origin, mass media have been created with the function of informing people, and it is quite natural that, depending on how information is presented to citizens, they will form their own opinions on the facts and events brought to their attention. With the breakthroughs in technology that characterised the first quarter of this century, the shaping potential of news has sharply increased, and the latest developments in artificial intelligence have made the functioning of this mechanism even more complex.

In order to give an idea of how the spread of news and the communication between public authorities and citizens can shape public opinion, we can easily mention the approach of the US mass media after the 9/11 attacks. At that time, the events were promptly labelled by President George W. Bush as a 'declaration' of war, entailing a full-fledged conflict, and the US media immediately echoed that statement, which started being repeated as a mantra in the ears of US citizens,[1] and this highly contributed to fuelling the 'patriotic' vein of US people against terrorists and to shaping the narrative of the 'war on terror', which even crossed US boundaries. On one side, this may be seen as a reasonable nudge to avoid the pitfalls of radicalisation; on the other, it encouraged the posture that tended to justify those warlike measures, which often infringed on basic human rights.[2]

[1] Rafat Mahmood and Michael Jetter, 'Communications Technology and Terrorism' (2020) 64 Journal of Conflicts Resolution 127; Amy Gershkoff and Shana Kushner, 'Shaping Public Opinion: The 9/11-Iraq Connection in the Bush Administration's Rhetoric' (2005) 3 Perspectives on Politics 525.

[2] Arianna Vedaschi, 'The Dark Side of Counter-Terrorism: The Argument for a More Enlightened Approach Based on a Constitutional Law

With artificial intelligence, the capacity of mass media and the news they share, as well as online platforms, to shape public opinion exponentially increased. It is enough to think of the ability of algorithms to profile our habits, preferences, the news we read, and thousands of other aspects of our lives to 'feed' us with the news that seems more appropriate according to our profiles. It can be easily understood how this mechanism can be exploited for very different aims.[3] From the perspective of governmental authorities, working in cooperation with non-profit entities and the tech industry, it can be used to build powerful counter-narratives, inducing citizens to reject terrorist ideologies and to categorise terrorist groups as negative actors.

In the following sections, we will first explain some case studies, drawing from the comparative scenario, where cutting-edge technologies are used to shape the opinion of the public with regard to the terrorist threat, sometimes intervening to try to block the radicalisation process; second, we will discuss the possible risks of these tools and their impact on rights and freedoms.

1. SHAPING PUBLIC OPINION AGAINST TERRORISM: SOME CASE-STUDIES FROM THE COMPARATIVE SCENARIO

Some of the most interesting case studies in this field have been surveyed by the Global Internet Forum to Counter Terrorism (GIFCT).[4] The GIFCT strongly contributed to enhancing several projects launched at the national and supranational levels and implying cooperation between

---

Paradigm', in Shimon Shetreet and Waine McCormak (eds), *The Culture of Judicial Independence in a Globalised World* (Brill-Nijhoff 2016) 94.

[3] Charis Rice, Martin Innes and Jenny Ratcliffe, 'Frame, Fame and Fear Traps: The Dialectic of Counter-Terrorism Strategic Communication' (2024) 47 Studies in Conflicts and Terrorism 1.

[4] The GIFCT gathers representatives of the technology industry, government, of civil society, and the scholarly environment in order to build effective collaboration and share information with a view to countering terrorism and extremist activities online. Chiara Graziani, 'Removing Terrorist Content Online. The Intersection between the International, Regional, and Domestic Level', in Arianna Vedaschi and Kim Lane Scheppele (eds), *9/11 and the Rise of Global Anti-Terrorism Law: How the UN Security Council Rules the World* (CUP 2021) 222.

national governments and the tech industry. These projects built systems that, also thanks to algorithms, can intervene with those who risk falling into radicalisation by offering them alternatives and/or explaining to them the perils of this path. In this context, an example is the project called Extreme Dialogue, developed by three non-profit organisations headquartered in both Europe and North America. Extreme Dialogue is based on an algorithm that spots online behaviour at risk of radicalisation and provides a link to a platform where people can dialogue with experts who explain the risks associated with extremism and nudge them towards better ways to express their personalities and find a role in society. This is a way to involve civil society and proceed through 'soft' measures rather than by directly resorting to stronger tools, such as criminal law.

Another method, called Redirect, works through targeted advertising containing counter-narrative. It has been developed by a UK company, Moonshot, in cooperation with Jigsaw, a Google subsidiary, and it is an open-source tool. The Redirect method is based on algorithms able to profile single users of the web and target this type of advertisement to those who reveal a radicalisation-prone pattern. Based on available data,[5] the Redirect method is widely used in Europe and the United States. It should be borne in mind that the initiative is totally in the hands of tech companies, not being the object of any hard law regulation; notwithstanding this, it should be noted that the European Union has included it among a 'collection of inspiring practices'[6] suggested by the Radicalisation Awareness Network (RAN).[7]

---

[5] Global Internet Forum to Counter Terrorism, 'Content-Sharing Algorithms, Processes, and Positive Interventions Working Group' (July 2021) https://gifct.org/wp-content/uploads/2021/07/GIFCT-CAPI2-2021.pdf accessed 31 July 2024. See also Radicalisation Awareness Network (RAN), 'Collection Practice Template. The Redirect Method' (2022) https://home-affairs.ec.europa.eu/document/download/26abaa70-2d4f-4637-add3-1bc66bcbd533_en?filename=redirect_methode_en.pdf. accessed 31 July 2024.

[6] European Commission, Migration and Home Affairs, The Redirect Method https://home-affairs.ec.europa.eu/networks/radicalisation-awareness-network-ran/collection-inspiring-practices/ran-practices/redirect-method-trm_en accessed 31 July 2024.

[7] The RAN is a network established at the European Union level, connecting practitioners, policymakers, and scholars who can cooperate to

Another relevant example in this field is YouTube's 'Featured Video' method. It works similarly to Redirect, with the difference that, instead of displaying advertisements, it shows counter-narrative videos. More specifically, when YouTube's algorithms identify some search keywords that could be symptomatic of a user at risk of radicalisation, it displays a list of alternative videos with content that strives to disengage the user from adherence to extremist narratives. This tool is available in all the countries having access to YouTube, hence it can be said to have an almost global reach.

In addition to these tools, many more could be mentioned. Some have a domestic reach (e.g. Canada-Redirect[8]); others are run by social media and tech companies (e.g. Meta's signposting initiatives[9]), so they are likely to reach a broad audience at least in theory. They all have in common at least three features. First, they are strongly grounded on intelligent algorithms, able to recognise dangerous features in the behaviour of users, although they are not free from mistakes and biased assessments; thus, this side could be tricky for human rights and personal freedoms. Second, they result from cooperation between the tech industry and non-profit organisations, sometimes with the involvement or support of national governments. Therefore, the strong public-private interplay pointed out in other parts of the book can be detected in this regard, too. And third, they are based on the mechanism of counter-narrative, which is proposed to users with a view to nudging them towards a different vision, something which, as anticipated, constitutes a 'softer' approach when compared with criminal law.

2. SHAPING THE PUBLIC OPINION AGAINST TERRORISM: POSSIBLE RISKS

The explained methods could seem very beneficial in the countering and prevention of terrorism from several perspectives. For example, they

---

frame counter-radicalisation practices that can work as policy suggestions.

8 See Moonshot, 'Redirect Method Canada' (March 2021) https://moonshotteam.com/wp-content/uploads/Final-Public-Report_Canada-Redirect_English.pdf accessed 31 July 2024.

9 This method sends people who search for terms associated with extremism on Facebook Search to web pages focused on helping people abandon extremist ideologies.

enter into function very quickly, as soon as a 'suspect' search on the internet is identified. Moreover, they also act on the sociological and psychological sides of the phenomenon of radicalisation, by dissuading people from getting involved in it, so it can be said that they intervene 'at the roots' of radicalisation, rather than by repressing single conduct. Additionally, their reach is potentially pervasive, as they are often developed by or in cooperation with big companies whose platforms extend all over the world, and they could be mentioned as examples of 'transnational' measures.

Notwithstanding these 'bright' sides, there are also some risks stemming from the use of algorithms to shape the opinion of citizens. We identified three categories of risks: the first category concerns the effectiveness of these methods; the second has to do with potentially excessive interference with some rights and freedoms; and the third is focussed on the dangers of abuse.

Starting from the first category, we do not want to discuss to what extent counter-narratives are effective on the minds of users, since those considerations are better left to sociological and psychological studies;[10] however, we cannot but notice that there are practical elements of these strategies that could impair their effectiveness. For example, if we take Redirect, it works by displaying targeted advertisements; nonetheless, there is no certainty that the user will click on those advertisements and thus be exposed to its counter-narrative. Something similar can be said with regard to the YouTube mechanism explained *supra*, since users are proposed to watch counter-narrative videos without being obliged (and actually they could not be obliged). Indeed, these worries are supported by some data provided by the same platforms, showing low click rates on these contents.[11]

Shifting to problems connected with the interference with some human rights, some introductory remarks are necessary. When we think of these strategies, impacting people's opinions, we usually deem them 'soft' measures, not entailing a strong invasion of people's rights; this is also why we tend to accept that they might not be fully effective (see

---

[10] Joshua Sinai, Jeffrey Fuller and Tiffany Seal, 'Effectiveness in Counter-Terrorism and Countering Violent Extremism: A Literature Review' (2019) 13 Perspectives on Terrorism 90.

[11] See data available in Global Internet Forum to Counter-Terrorism, *op. cit.*, 21.

immediately *supra*). Though the situation could be read in a different way upon closer inspection. The fact that these tools are able to target advertisements and contents and shape them according to users' searches means that they perform fully-fledged surveillance on what users are doing on their devices, their habits and their preferences. This is undoubtedly a form of mass surveillance, carried out primarily by private entities. Not only does this feature engage the usual privacy considerations, e.g. the need for consent, but it also implies that this data becomes the object of potential commercial transactions, as well as exchanges with other parties (e.g. foreign intelligence).

The last, but no less important, category of risks concerns potential abuses. In order to train the algorithm to recognise potential risky behaviour in terms of terrorist radicalisation and violent extremism, the algorithm itself should be trained to recognise terrorist narratives, or at least their 'symptoms'. It is evident how this feature could be instrumentalised in illiberal contexts, for instance by training an algorithm to label mere political dissent or journalists' work as 'terrorism'. In this regard, the case law of the European Court of Human Rights,[12] which is very developed around the use of counter-terrorism to repress dissent, might give some guidance but would not solve the problem as a whole. This is especially true because, most of the time, these algorithms are the object of intellectual property rights or are shielded by trade secrets, so it remains mostly unknown how they are designed and work. For this reason, assessing whether or not they are instrumentalised to quell political or other forms of dissent might prove challenging both for courts and public opinion. In other words, the lack of transparency is not helpful in terms of democratic oversight over the functioning of the algorithm.

[12] See, among others, European Court of Human Rights, *Sahin Alpay v. Turkey*, app. no. 16538/17, 20 March 2018.

A final overview on technology as a counter-terrorism tool

In Part II we have provided an analysis of the several ways in which technology has been used for counter-terrorism purposes, and how these tools have evolved. We have highlighted several times that some techniques started as merely 'automated' systems and then benefited from artificial intelligence, thus becoming 'autonomous' ones.

In this final overview of Part II, we want to remark on three common traits of all the technologies that we surveyed, which will be useful to then develop the concluding remarks of the book as a whole.

The first common aspect, which we have pointed out throughout Part II and deserves to be stressed once again, is the tight interplay between public authorities and private entities. The more advanced algorithms and other techniques are, the stronger the reliance of public authorities on private companies will be. This is not, of course the first case of so-called public-private partnership, since we can mention several previous examples in other fields, spanning from the hybrid management of some public resources, to public finance, to some other sectors of economics. However, this approach in the area of national security and regarding such cutting-edge technologies combines two challenging issues: on one side, the sensitivity of national security; on the other, the fact that these technologies are far from being fully consolidated, as they are updated day by day thanks to new breakthroughs.

The second common feature is that the private bodies that own these technologies and cooperate with the public bodies are often extremely reluctant to comply with the principle of transparency, which is a basic element in any rule of law-grounded legal system. Non-disclosure of certain details of one's activity is common for market operators, who are bound by intellectual property and copyright law. Nevertheless, this perspective may clash with the fact that national security is one of the fields where the trust relationship between public authorities and civil society is 'tested' more intensely. Denying access to these details impairs this relationship and hinders the legislative activity.

Here comes the third common characteristic. The continuous evolution, along with the fact that sometimes it is difficult to understand how these technologies work since their functioning is not disclosed by their owners, causes a systematic and chronic delay for lawmakers at all levels in regulating the matter. If, on the one hand, law is normally an *ex post facto* phenomenon, so this delay might not be worrying, it is also true, on the other hand, that the distance between the advancement of technology and the existing regulation is beginning to become excessive. We will get back to this topic as one of the points of the conclusions of the book, in order to suggest some guidelines on how lawmakers could regain momentum without renouncing the performances that technology guarantees.

Appendix to Part II

Table A2.1 Technology as a counter-terrorist tool

Identification of the threat and assessment of the risk
In synthesis: Tools aimed at understanding whether or not a certain person, fact or event represents a terrorist risk. Tools: • Metadata surveillance (often resorting to 'algorithmic surveillance tools'); • Algorithms to flag terrorist content online; • Facial recognition tools.
Chasing the threat
In synthesis: Tools aimed at investigating someone who is already at least suspected as a terrorist; sometimes, these tools even target those who have already been convicted as terrorists. Tools: • Mechanisms for individual interception (different degrees of advancement, see focus on spyware); • 'Smart prisons'.
Shaping public opinion
In synthesis: Tools aimed at fueling people's sentiment against terrorism or at preventing individuals from becoming radicalised (counter-radicalisation/prevention of radicalisation). Tools: • Online and offline press; • Redirect methods; • Ad hoc advertisements.

Conclusions: artificial intelligence in the field of security – rule of law concerns, regulatory challenges and geopolitical impact

Our book has delved into the intersection of three main topics, namely: technology, in its most advanced form represented by artificial intelligence; security, especially with regard to counter-terrorism measures; and the respect for human rights, an essential feature of the rule of law.

The joint and analytical reading of these three major topics brought us to point out some findings emerging from single chapters, converging towards some common issues that deserve further consideration in the conclusive part of this work.

These crucial matters can be classified into three general categories: the substantive ones, in terms of the security-rights relationship; the regulatory ones, i.e., those having an impact on the regulatory framework, particularly tricky in the artificial intelligence field; and those with a geopolitical scope. In the following sections, we examine those topics according to this categorisation.

1. SUBSTANTIVE ISSUES

Starting from substantive issues, which go to the core of the complex relationship between technology, security and rights, we identified two main points potentially having effects also on artificial intelligence in its broader scope and its impact on rights. The first point is how the concept of security is changing in the current scenario, while the second point concerns the new challenges that the 'guardians' of the balance between security and rights have to face in this new digital background. Traditionally, these guardians are considered to be the courts, but in our book we made reference to other actors as well (see *infra*).

First, we can focus on the change in the idea of security. There are several clues that this concept might be undergoing a metamorphosis, at least from a European viewpoint. Along with other matters, it was very clear that national security fell outside of EU competences. This exemption of national security matters from EU law seems no longer so clear-cut. As a matter of fact, if we look at some recent pieces of EU legislation, we see that, by regulating the field of law enforcement (i.e., public security and public order), the EU institutions *de facto* intervene in areas that fall within the scope of national security, such as counter-terrorism. With the AI Act,[1] we have a patent example: if one looks at Recital 24, it states that '[…] AI systems […] for military, defence or national security purposes […] should be excluded from the scope of this Regulation'; yet Article 5(h)(ii), in affirming that real-time biometric systems can be deployed for counter-terrorism purposes, indeed legislates on national security matters, since terrorism consists of a threat coming externally against the State, at least in its international dimension, or anyway in activities causing serious harm to citizens and institutions as well as a perception of insecurity among civil society. Here, we can uncontestably see how national security is embedded into public security.

Another trace of this conflation between public and national security can be found in the norms of Regulation (EU) 2021/784, on terrorist content online. This regulation is enacted on the legal basis of Article 114 of the Treaty on the Functioning of the European Union (TFEU), regarding the approximation of rules in the internal market, and its provisions only mention law enforcement activities, so there is no explicit reference to national security. However, it is very evident that, by laying down common rules for law enforcement that have an impact on the common market, this piece of legislation is having an influence on how Member States manage their national security policies. In fact, cooperating with internet service providers to remove posts regarding international terrorism coincides with defending the internal dimension of the State from external menaces or attempts at destabilisation.

These are only a couple of cases when we can plainly see an overlap between national and public security, as further examples could be found, e.g., in the field of privacy legislation, but they are indicative of a trend in the European Union. As a matter of fact, this conflation between these two notions might have important systemic consequences, as the

[1] Regulation (EU) 2024/1689.

EU might expand its role more and more. Among others, it might start reclaiming a stronger voice in military matters, although the provisions of the Treaties exclude this area, by exploiting a 'grey zone' in the interpretation of its competences. In addition, from a more theoretical perspective, the intersection between public security and national security may imply a change in the notion of sovereignty or, more clearly, a concealed – meaning, without any change in the Treaties – increase in the amount of sovereignty shifted from Member States to the EU institutions.

From our viewpoint, although the European Union's attempt to indirectly regulate the field of national security through other competences may negatively impact the principle of attribution, the push towards the supranational dimension is not surprising. Threats such as terrorism go beyond the national dimension, and so it might prove necessary to reinterpret the traditional view, according to which national security only pertains to State sovereignty, on the basis of new schemes. This dynamic manifestly points out the growing transnational dimension of security, which in turn joins the already consolidated transnational nature of technology, a point that we will develop in section 2.

The second substantive question that we anticipated at the beginning of this section deals with the role of the traditional 'guardians' (i.e., the courts) tasked with assessing the complex balance between rights and security when technology is at stake. In general, striking a fair balance between security and rights has been a serious issue at least since the 9/11 events. In this context, courts have always played a leading role in determining the right combination of these two factors in specific cases. The case law on the principle of proportionality, which is very well-developed in supranational judicial bodies when security comes into play, confirms this statement. However, in the 'digital era', some issues are arising and making things more challenging. The first challenge is that the proportionality assessment is increasingly complicated by technical factors depending on algorithmic mechanisms, which sometimes are even undisclosed, due to industrial secrets, intellectual property rights, and other similar issues concerning market operators, if not because of technical reasons impairing the principle of transparency.

Another point that touches upon the courts is that, as observed by some scholars,[2] in the new digital world, already existing rights are taking

---

[2] Carlo Casonato, 'Artificial Intelligence and (Old and New) Human Rights' (2023) 3 Biolaw Journal 233; Philipp Hacker, 'Comments on the

on new dimensions. A well-working example is the right to receive an explanation of algorithmic processes, which stems from the principle of transparency but might prove difficult to apply when black box algorithms are resorted to. These new dimensions of 'old' rights could pose some problems of coordination with pre-existing case law and established standards of courts, which might need to be revised.

A last, and probably more worrying issue is that, in the current scenario, the oversight of the courts is sometimes replaced either by an ad hoc body, meaning independent administrative authorities, or even by boards established within the tech company itself, such as the Meta Oversight Board that we mentioned in Chapter 4. The latter are totally private bodies, without any public legitimation, since they are appointed by companies according to their own mechanisms. This trend causes an increase in the problems of independence in abstract terms, along with issues of accessibility of decisions and prompt reviewability of decisions. In fact, after a case has been adjudicated by these bodies, the path towards courts might be delayed, complicated, and often there are no guarantees that all technical issues will be assessed properly.

We do acknowledge that independent administrative authorities may play a role in *ex ante* oversight, as widely recognised in EU law, since they may ensure quicker action and more technical assessment of the matter; nonetheless, in no case should they be involved in *ex post* review, since this would result in a serious violation of the separation of powers as well as the principle of judicial independence. *A fortiori*, boards established by big tech companies lack the necessary guarantees to take a final decision; they might work well, also in light of their technical expertise, to give a first assessment of the situation and provide a non-binding opinion, but we argue that final judgment should always remain in the hands of an independent judiciary power. In our view, when the balance between security and rights is concerned in specific cases – and hence legislation needs to be concretely applied – the courts are and remain the most appropriate actors to assess single situations, strike a balance, and take a decision for those individual cases, including in contexts where technology plays a relevant role. In order to enhance the role of courts, even in the most advanced digital era, i.e., that of artificial intelligence, we suggest that higher transparency requirements – not only in terms of reporting but also including notice on how their algorithms

Final Trilogue Version of the AI Act', 23 January 2024.

are programmed and work – should be imposed on companies, and this should be done through binding legislation, overstepping, when needed, IP rights and trade secrets.

At the same time, judges' and other practitioners' training should be improved, and this is a very important aspect that sometimes tends to be sidelined in the debate about these matters. Instead, it is crucial that they are made aware at least of the basic notions of how algorithms function, thus making their education more interdisciplinary than it is at present. Still with a view to merging the legal and technical dimensions, essential to ensure fair and well-thought-out judgments, the hearing of independent experts might help as well. Courts around the world have several mechanisms at their disposal to allow the hearing of experts, and they might exploit them more and more for this purpose.

2. REGULATORY ISSUES

As anticipated at the beginning of this conclusive chapter, the considerations that we would like to make do not regard only substantive matters but also some regulatory issues pertaining to a more formal perspective. These two dimensions – substantive and regulatory/formal – are far from being separated because some substantive topics might be differently impacted and handled depending on the chosen regulatory approach.

Regulatory issues can be defined as all those matters related to whether (and, if so, to what extent) legal regulation is necessary in the area of artificial intelligence, especially when it is applied to security, and which bodies are to be considered better placed to draw up such a regulatory framework. These are indeed very general issues, which could be discussed with regard to any use of artificial intelligence – meaning, not necessarily in the field of counter-terrorism; nevertheless, there are some peculiarities with reference to security that we highlight in this section, when necessary.

The first point – is regulation necessary, and if so, to what degree? – is definitely a crucial topic. We need to understand that law usually comes *after* phenomena take place and develop. In other words, any legal rule is characterised by an *ex post* nature. In the case of technology, the *ex post* nature of law makes the scenario particularly challenging. As a matter of fact, technology evolves in an extremely rapid manner, much faster than many other phenomena, and so legal regulation risks being outdated from its very origin; some scholars have even talked about a 'promethean gap'.[3] Security makes things even more complicated, as terrorists strive to keep their strategies, plans, and targets as hidden as possible, making it is very difficult to devise effective and updated countermeasures.

When it comes to the challenging issue of deciding whether and how to regulate technology, in general and in the field of security, we face several options. A first option can be defined as the 'zero option' and corresponds to no regulation at all, or, rather, no regulation enacted by public bodies, meaning those that we are used to considering as the traditional regulators, such as lawmakers, governmental bodies, etc. This stance leaves everything to market dynamics, hence it entails that big techs become the real rulers. This market-oriented approach is typical of the United States and has been pointed out several times throughout our book. Let us just think of the very tolerant and libertarian posture that they take towards the moderation of dangerous content online, reinforced by recent case law of the federal Supreme Court. Leaving so much discretion to the market and its operators undoubtedly favours innovation, as the industry is left free to experiment, trial, and develop its own tools, at the expense or even to the detriment of other interests. And this may happen, as this book showed, even when the other interest is a public one, such as national security. Again, the example of the moderation or, rather in this case, no moderation of terrorist content online in the US context is illustrative, since big tech companies are always considered not liable in an effort to guarantee both free enterprise from the perspective of companies and free speech from the viewpoint of users, yet to the detriment of security, as the web may become a dangerous place, potentially filled with radicalising content.

A second option is a sort of middle ground path between regulation and non-regulation. It consists of refraining from issuing ad hoc regulation, but rather relying on general legal principles to solve specific problems. In favour of this approach, one can mention the argument according to which general principles are quite flexible, and they might

[3] Massimo Luciani, *Le sfide dell'intelligenza artificiale*, Associazione Italiana dei Costituzionalisti, 2023, https://www.associazionedeicostituzionalisti.it/it/la-lettera/12-2023-liberta-di-ricerca-e-intelligenza-artificiale/la-sfida-dell-intelligenza-artificiale accessed 31 July 2024. Translation by authors (Italian expression: 'dislivello prometeico'). This expression is actually taken from Günther Anders, talking about 'prometeische Gefälle' between technical (and technological) research and its practical application.

be more likely, compared to detailed rules, to keep pace with the fast and unstoppable development of technology. More than by lawmakers, this approach, grounded on general principles, has often been used by some courts dealing with technology issues that were not properly regulated at the time of their judgment. The field of security made no exception in this regard: let us consider the *La Quadrature du Net* and *Privacy International* cases,[4] when the European Court of Justice addressed algorithmic surveillance at a time when neither the regulation on terrorist content online nor the AI Act was yet in force, and so the judges tried to deal with algorithmic matters by applying general principles arising from the Charter of Fundamental Rights of the European Union and from their own previous case law. This interpretative technique resulted in the application of the proportionality principle in a way that makes it updated to new innovations brought by algorithmic surveillance.

A third possible path, then, embodies the general regulation of the field. This has been defined by scholars as the 'horizontal approach'[5] and means that the whole subject is regulated without providing specific and differentiated rules for the application of the tool to different fields – in this case, artificial intelligence. This is exactly what the European Union has done with Regulation (EU) 2024/1689 (the AI Act), since, as remarked in this volume, it is an omni-comprehensive piece of legislation, largely based on the 'one size fits all' logic. It is true that it poses some rules applicable to specific sectors – see, e.g., the use of biometric data in law enforcement activities – but they are still within the wider context of the general regulation, and they merely constitute an exception to general rules, rather than a full, complete, and separate legal framework addressing law enforcement and biometric algorithms. The choice made by the European Union to embrace this horizontal approach can undoubtedly be traced back to its will to affirm itself as a leader in the regulation of artificial intelligence as a general and global phenomenon.

Along with the horizontal approach, a further possible regulatory strategy – the fourth option in our list – can be the 'vertical' one. By

[4] European Court of Justice (Grand Chamber), *La Quadrature du Net and Others v Premier ministre and Others*, Case C-511/18, 6 October 2020; Id., *Privacy International v Secretary of State for Foreign and Commonwealth Affairs and Others*, Case C-623/17.

[5] Giusella Finocchiaro, 'The Regulation of Artificial Intelligence' (2023) AI & Society 1.

this expression, we mean that another possibility is to envisage separate regulatory frameworks for each field in which artificial intelligence is deployed, from security – the centre of our work – to many others, such as contracts, administrative tasks, etc. This stance, which can also be defined as a sectorial one, has been advocated by some international organisations,[6] as it might allegedly ensure more specific, detailed, and easily enforceable rules. In other terms, it would prevent normative gaps and provide practitioners (judges, officials, etc.) with rules ready to be applied, limiting the room for doubts and interpretation. We can actually see a trace of this approach, with regard to security issues, taking into account the EU regulation on terrorist content online, namely Regulation (EU) 2021/784.[7] Nonetheless, as said, a few years later the European Union had already changed its focus, at least partially, preferring a general – or horizontal – approach (reference is to what has been said *supra* with regard to the very recent AI Act). Among the reasons that may have pushed the European Union to abandon vertical regulation is that the more specific the rules are, the more likely it is that they become outdated very early. Therefore, preference for horizontal regulation may be considered an attempt to preserve enacted legal rules through time, preventing them from becoming obsolete. However, in thorny topics such as security, keeping some vertical regulation might be useful, as we will argue in the remainder of this section.

The fifth and last option, as far as the regulation of artificial intelligence is concerned, has not been directly addressed in this book, if not through some hints, but is worth mentioning in these concluding considerations, since it provides food for thought on the topics we are examining. Reference is to a type of intrusive and hyper-detailed regulation, typical of systems like China, focussed on how the State (or, anyway, public authorities) has to interact with the big tech industry, so there is indeed a change of topic compared to previous approaches. If adopted in a non-democratic environment and pushed to the extreme, this stance brings the idea of technology as a shortcut to manage the economy and

---

[6] See the UNIDROIT-UNCITRAL Joint Workshop on smart contracts, artificial intelligence, and distributed ledger technology, held in Rome at the International Institute for the Unification of Private Law (Unidroit) on 6–7 May 2019.

[7] See Chapter 5 of the Book.

ultimately control society.[8] This posture bears several elements of dirigisme, insofar as State authorities vest themselves with the power to prohibit access to some networks or information. Often such prohibitions are made exactly on the basis of national security considerations, and the exploitation of these grounds to curb political dissent occurs frequently.

Given this overview of possible ways to regulate artificial intelligence, both in general and with specific reference to security, it is worth analysing which one(s), among these options, might be feasible in order to guarantee security while at the same time safeguarding human rights and the rule of law.

In our view, resorting to what we have called the 'zero option', coinciding with no or poor regulation to favor a market-oriented approach – as happens in the United States – is risky from the perspective of individual rights. In fact, market operators, such as the big tech companies, are not the best-placed actors to ensure the protection of rights, particularly when they need to be weighed against such a serious and sensitive interest as security. Moreover, it is our opinion that such a stance may create serious normative gaps when cases come before the courts since judges cannot apply the policies or terms of services of the providers as if they were law, simply because they are not such and thus do not have normative force. Consequently, we argue that leaving the topic totally in the hands of the tech industry cannot be the best solution and that while companies should retain some discretion on certain specific technical matters, these should be exceptions limited to detailed and particular aspects and not result in general policy choices. Regarding security, this point is extremely important since private companies cannot take over public authorities in a field that represents one of the biggest public interests.

The second option that we envisaged has to do with the application of general principles to infer how technology should be regulated, in general and in the area of security. This option could be a viable and useful possibility for courts when they have to solve a practical case and they do not have any normative basis, but it cannot become the general rule and, most of all, it cannot be considered as the primary available tool from the perspective of lawmakers. In other words, reliance on existing general principles is not a definitive solution to regulate technology, since general principles are open to very different interpretations, potentially

[8] Anu Bradford, *Digital Empires* (OUP 2023) 69.

changing on the basis of the political, social, and economic scenario, and this does not always ensure certainty of law and legality, two key principles which contribute to the concept of rule of law[9] that we address in this work. Therefore, general principles – often subject to analogical interpretations – can be a last resort in practical cases, to fill in normative gaps by judicial authorities, and should only exceptionally be used in the lawmaking domain.

Another path that we do not definitely support is the State-driven approach, which we described as typical of the Chinese legal system. This posture is too prone to abuse in non-democratic scenarios, and it could even enhance democratic decay in other political contexts, turning them into non-democratic countries. In fact, a State-based approach excludes, or at least sidelines, human rights and personal freedoms, which cease to be among the main actors in the discourse regarding technology and security. Additionally, if technology is functionalised to the State and to the flourishing of the economy, there is no longer a separation between the State and the market, and this is normally a feature leading to undemocratic paths. Last but not least, the fact that many impositions by the State are made based on alleged national security considerations might turn out to be a populist way to manipulate people, another dangerous dynamic from the perspective of maintaining democracy.

At this point, we can focus on which options we consider viable, both in terms of general regulation and specifically for security. In this regard,

[9] As known, the rule of law is a very complex and multifaceted concept, with a long historical background. In order to simplify it and make its standards immediately understandable, the Venice Commission has adopted a 'rule of law checklist', revolving around six macro-standards that are considered essential to consider any legal context as rule-of-law-based. These are (listed in this order): the principle of legality, including transparency of applicable rules; the principle of legal certainty, extending to the need to clearly identifying someone who bears the responsibility for certain acts; the prohibition of arbitrariness; the right of access to justice; the respect for human rights in general, in which the Commission explicitly includes compliance with the presumption of innocence; and, last but not least, the principle of non-discrimination and equality before the law. European Commission for Democracy through Law (Venice Commission), Report on the Rule of Law, adopted by the Venice Commission at its 86th plenary session, Venice, 25–26 March 2011 https://www.venice.coe.int/webforms/documents/?pdf=CDL-AD(2011)003rev-e accessed 31 July 2024.

we do think that a certain degree of regulation in the field of artificial intelligence is necessary, and that this applies also with reference to its security uses. The efforts of the European Union in passing the AI Act, as well as other legislation we have mentioned throughout the book, deserve to be praised; however, a certain lack of specific rules for individual sectors is worrying, as this may impair the protection of rights. We do not want to argue that the EU should enact legislation for any of the (almost endless) fields in which artificial intelligence can be used; rather, to the general framework posed through the AI Act, more detailed sub-frameworks should follow, at least in critical areas such as security and counter-terrorism. We then welcome the AI Act as a first step, but we encourage further, sectorial moves since we think that the horizontal and vertical approaches are not necessarily mutually exclusive; on the contrary, they can co-exist if we consider the AI Act as a general framework, to which more detailed rules on security can be added, working like a sort of *lex specialis*. Specifically, it would be useful to enact pieces of legislation that do more than just pose exceptions to allow prohibitions to be overstepped on the grounds of counter-terrorism action; it would be crucial to indicate stricter rules on what can be considered as a threat to security, what is the threshold to activate the related regulation, and what caveats should be observed by those who programme algorithms for use in this field. We are aware that such a goal cannot be achieved immediately, and that several years of trials and adjustments might be necessary; however, we deem it important to emphasise this as a possible right direction for future lawmakers.

Another noteworthy point, which we want to highlight, is that potential EU legislative developments on security would need to find 'indirect' legal bases, such as the internal market or law enforcement activities, because, as we pointed out *supra*, national security is so far exempted from the scope of EU law. Although this is not an ideal path and we do not recommend it in absolute terms, since indirectly regulating something that is out of the scope of EU competences may create uncertainty, grey zones and formal criticalities, as hinted above, this is the only feasible route at the present time.

Once these considerations about whether and to what extent artificial intelligence needs to be regulated, even when security comes into play, we can shift to some stimulating reflections regarding who is better placed to regulate such a complicated field. Said in another way, after we have delved into the dimension of the regulatory matters, we have to focus on the subjective one.

The answer about who is best placed to regulate technology depends, at least to some extent, on the answer about the desired degree of regulation with which we dealt *supra*. As a matter of fact, the subjective regulators change a lot depending on the chosen approach to technology regulation. For instance, where a market-oriented approach is adopted, the regulators cannot but be tech companies; the latter remain key actors when reliance is made on general principles, with the only difference being that their policies and terms of services are interpreted based on these principles, and so there is a slightly stronger role of the public sector, although in the guise of a judge, rather than a lawmaker. The other approaches pointed out *supra*, instead, see a stronger role of traditional regulators, i.e., public authorities. Such a role is more balanced in the case of a horizontal or vertical regulatory approach – that we have exemplified through the European Union legislation – while it is at its peak if we take into account the dirigiste model, which represents the degenerated example of public regulation.

From our perspective, looking at big tech as 'the evil' in the regulation of technology would not be a feasible choice nor would it be in line with the reality of the existing scenario. What, in our view, should be avoided is that these companies are the only or the leading regulators of the field. We argue in favor of cooperation based on a coordinating role of public powers and a supporting role of private actors, which could be carried out, e.g., through controlled forms of lobbying or ad hoc consultations. Private actors need to be involved in the decision-making process aimed at adopting legally binding acts, but the core of these acts should be in the hands of public powers, especially when security is at stake, due to the high relevance of the latter as a key public interest. Looking at existing experiences, we see that such a fair balance between the public and the private sphere has hardly ever been reached, since the examples that we have at our disposal – including at the European level – still leave a significant margin of discretion to the tech industry, which, as we have highlighted in the chapters of the book, is eroding some of the most important public functions and even, to some degree, the idea of sovereignty. Once again, the case of moderation policies adopted by tech industries to prevent dangerous content is illustrative.

In sum, the public-private relationship in this field should be public-led rather than private-led, although the proactive role of private bodies should be guaranteed. As hinted, this statement is even more important with regard to the application of artificial intelligence to security, because security is normally better managed by public authorities, since it can be encompassed in the notion of public well-being, toward which public action should mainly be directed.

In the process of decision-making aimed at enacting regulation, not only big public and private entities, but also single individuals making up the civil society, should be involved in a meaningful way. Including civil society – thus framing a partially bottom-up, and not only top-down, approach – is essential to put enacted laws into existing reality and ensure smoother compliance. This aspect has been criticised by some scholars[10] regarding the AI Act, which has been claimed to have been adopted without a sufficient degree of public consultation, to the detriment of democratic standards. At the same time, according to the mentioned scholars, the AI Act does not ensure sufficient involvement of civil society in the review of AI systems aimed at scoring their risk, which would have been another pivotal tool for keeping them active parts of the process.

Still within the topic of who should rule technology, another central issue is which level(s) of government is (are) better placed to regulate this matter. Until this moment, the supranational one – namely, the European Union – has proved to be the most effective, since at least it passed some rules applicable on a large scale. The prominence of the supranational level is coherent with the patent 'transnational' character of technology, which, as hinted in the previous section, tends to escape by its very nature national boundaries and jurisdictions. The same transnational dimension was not shared, at least traditionally, by the concept of security, which was born as something strongly attached to the idea of national sovereignty. Nonetheless, at least since 2001, security has been assuming increasingly global features, as the threats loom over the world as a whole, and international terrorism is among the most patent examples; the global dimension of the threat cannot but result in the need for a transnational approach in countermeasures. Exactly in the light of this necessary transnational reach, some voices[11] have claimed that, at any

[10] Nathalie Smuha et al., 'How the EU Can Achieve Legally Trustworthy AI: A Response to the European Commission's Proposal for an Artificial Intelligence Act', LEADS Lab Papers @University of Birmingham, for a Legal, Ethical and Accountable Digital Society, 5 August 2021 https://papers.ssrn.com/sol3/papers.cfm?abstract_id=3899991 accessed 31 July 2024.

[11] European Parliament Research Service, Regulating Facial Recognition in the EU, PE 698.021, September 2021 https://www.europarl.europa.eu

rate when security is concerned, international law could play a role as well, e.g., in the form of bilateral or multilateral agreements. We do think that involvement of the international level – which, so far, has proved quite ineffective, also due to single States' reluctance to engage in cooperation – would be more than welcome, but the risk of fragmentation, which lurks most of all behind bilateral agreements, should be avoided, e.g., by preferring multilateral and potentially slower cooperation to bilateral although quicker forms.

3. GEOPOLITICAL ISSUES

The third area that we deem essential to analyse regards geopolitical issues arising from recent developments in the legal framework regulating technology. Observations on the geopolitical sphere are momentous in the field of security, which is per se a geopolitical question, characterised by a transnational reach.

From this geopolitical angle, the first point that deserves consideration is the so-called Brussels effect,[12] i.e., the tendency of the European Union to achieve, *de jure* and *de facto*, extra-territorial application of its rules in order to become an influential actor and give shape to the world in its image, meaning that it tries to push third countries towards its values, or at least towards convergent rights protection standards. This aspiration has been very distinct in the field of privacy and data protection, and it is much more tangible with regard to artificial intelligence, as the European Union is trying to affirm itself as the regulator par excellence of the matter to which the whole world should conform. In the area of security, this feature stands out, since the European Union is the only actor that has at least provided some binding rules on how artificial intelligence should be handled. Against this background, we might wonder what the consequences of the Brussels effect will be in the geopolitical scenario and whether this effect is actually as strong as it is claimed to be.

A second issue that deserves to be addressed in this part dedicated to geopolitical aspects is related to the strength of the Brussels effect and

/RegData/etudes/IDAN/2021/698021/EPRS_IDA(2021)698021_EN.pdf accessed 31 July 2024.

[12] Anu Bradford, *The Brussels Effect: How the European Union Rules the World* (OUP 2020).

consists of dwelling on whether a 'winning model' on the regulation of technology, with specific regard to security, will ever exist.

Starting from the first topic, i.e., the reach of the Brussels effect in the field of artificial intelligence and security, there is no doubt that, so far, the AI Act is the only comprehensive framework to regulate artificial intelligence; similarly, the EU regulation on terrorist content online has a wide territorial application *de jure* that may expand *de facto*. Moreover, both these tools have an extra-territorial scope, insofar as they apply to companies not based in the European Union, though acting within the EU jurisdiction or just deploying their content thereof. Therefore, the European Union is definitely trying to impose itself as a transboundary regulator on technology in general as well as on the balance between security and rights when technology is at stake, thus giving rise to transnationally enforceable legal rules.

From a more general perspective, we can stress the transnational dimension, which comes back again and transversally cross-cuts all of the three areas that we addressed in these concluding remarks. Thanks to its transnational efforts, the European Union aims at pushing other actors, most of all US companies, to renounce the market based approach and comply with the same legal rules, in spite of the fact that they are not based in any EU Member State.

This ambition of the European Union is an effective one if we consider that, so far, it has been the only actor to engage in attempts at regulation. We are indeed aware that some scholars[13] warned that the strength of the Brussels effect should be downsized, maintaining that it is not as strong as depicted. For instance, they argued that this effect might be diminished by the force of other actors in play, namely the United States and China, not to mention the tech industry, which will tend to comply with EU rules only to the bare minimum, insofar as the existence of a legal framework means substantial financial costs[14] and the limitation of their discretion and, thereby, market power. Although we recognise that these

---

[13] See, e.g., Andrea Pin and Lucia Scaffardi, 'Tra protezione dei dati e intelligenza artificiale, in Europa e oltre', DPCE Online (2024).

[14] This aspect, seriously endangering the existence of small companies on the market, has also been highlighted also by Mario Draghi in a report to the European Commission on the competitiveness of the European Union. See Mario Draghi, 'The future of European competitiveness – In-depth analysis and recommendations', 9 September 2024.

arguments have a certain degree of foundation – since the political and normative force of the European Union cannot totally overstep the power of the jurisdictions of third countries as well as of the market, including the main tech companies – we think that the European Union has still achieved an unprecedented objective. This goal is that the efforts of the European Union through its regulation are having the effect of making some behaviour illegal, or on the edge of legality. That said, it is likely that companies will continue to perform some illegal conduct because it is economically convenient, or profitable, to do so and, in a risk-benefit analysis, they may prefer to risk sanctions rather than comply with EU legal rules. However, the existence and enforceability of legal rules represent an important milestone, and their application to such a transnational sector as technology results in an enhancement of the Brussels effect, which we deem very strong in this specific field. In the sectorial field of security, it is desirable that the Brussels effect is even enhanced, insofar as, among the models that we surveyed, the one developed – and still subject to improvement – by the European Union is the one that takes into higher consideration the balance between human rights and national/public security, although the alchemy between these two elements needs continuous monitoring, updating, and adjustment.

These remarks lead us directly toward the second and last point of these geopolitical insights, that is, whether there will ever be a 'winning model' in the regulation of technology. In this regard, as emerges from our previous analysis, there are at least two macro-models in the regulation of technology: the US market-oriented one and the European rights-oriented one. To these two paradigms, we can add the State-oriented model on which China is based, which, however, we have not addressed in detail in our book, since we focussed our study on Western democracies. We can wonder whether we are moving towards the prevalence of one of the two Western models.

According to our standpoint, the absolute prevalence of one or the other model is not foreseeable. It will very much depend on the political strength of the actors as well as on the social and economic context. An option could be the use of regulatory power to 'globalise' the European Union approach, which is more oriented towards individual rights than towards the market's interests – an aim pursued instead by the United States. An expansion of the European posture is desirable, although, as maintained in several parts of the book, we are aware that it can still be improved from several perspectives and that market and political forces might make it less straightforward, causing some ups and downs. In order to boost this challenging process, some steps could be taken. For instance, the enhancement of discussion fora among representatives of the European Union and third countries might be useful to foster a cultural change towards better extra-EU standards. In parallel, maximising the incentives (e.g., tax reliefs) for companies (including foreign ones) that deploy their services in the European Union and ensure compliance with sectorial legislation would be a way to compensate for the costs of compliance, which would otherwise make the EU market increasingly unattractive for third countries' industries.

From a general viewpoint, affirming a rights-oriented stance and working towards its improvement is crucial in general and in cases where security is at stake, to keep the right-security relationship within the framework of the rule of law.

Index